Building a Foundation for Preschool Literacy

Effective Instruction for Children's Reading and Writing Development

Carol Vukelich
University of Delaware
Newark, Delaware, USA

James Christie
Arizona State University
Tempe, Arizona, USA

EDITOR OF PRESCHOOL LITERACY COLLECTION
Lesley Mandel Morrow
Rutgers University
New Brunswick, New Jersey, USA

INTERNATIONAL
Reading Association
800 BARKSDALE ROAD, PO BOX 8139
NEWARK, DE 19714-8139, USA
www.reading.org

KH

Director of Publications Joan M. Irwin
Editorial Director, Books and Special Projects Matthew W. Baker
Managing Editor Shannon Benner
Permissions Editor Janet S. Parrack
Acquisitions and Communications Coordinator Corinne M. Mooney
Associate Editor, Books and Special Projects Sara J. Murphy
Assistant Editor Charlene M. Nichols
Administrative Assistant Michele Jester
Senior Editorial Assistant Tyanna L. Collins
Production Department Manager Iona Muscella
Supervisor, Electronic Publishing Anette Schütz
Senior Electronic Publishing Specialist Cheryl J. Strum
Electronic Publishing Specialist R. Lynn Harrison
Proofreader Elizabeth C. Hunt

Project Editors Matthew W. Baker and Shannon Benner

Freelance Editor Susan Hodges

Cover Design Linda Steere

Library of Congress Cataloging-in-Publication Data

Vukelich, Carol.
    Building a foundation for preschool literacy : effective instruction for children's reading and writing development / Carol Vukelich, James Christie.
        p. cm.
    Includes bibliographical references and index.
    ISBN 0-87207-547-8
    1. Language arts (Preschool).   I. Christie, James F.   II. Title.
    LB1140.5.L3V83 2004
    372.6--dc22
                                                                                    2004005473

Fifth Printing, February 2006

10/19/06

CONTENTS

GLOSSARY

The following glossary provides definitions for many of the specialized literacy terms in this book. These terms are highlighted in boldface type the first time they appear in each chapter.

assessment: Gathering relevant information to document a child's learning and growth.

concepts of print: Children's understandings about the functions (e.g., practical uses), structure (e.g., printed words are separated by spaces), and conventions (e.g., left-to-right, top-to-bottom sequence) of written language.

dialogic reading: An interactive form of storybook reading in which an adult helps a child become the storyteller.

dramatic play: An advanced form of play in which children take on roles and act out make-believe stories and situations.

emergent literacy: A perspective on early literacy development that contends that children construct their own knowledge about reading and writing as a result of social interaction and meaningful engagements with print.

environmental print: The print children see at home or in the community, including print on food containers and other kinds of product boxes, store signs, road signs, and advertisements.

evidence-based reading research (EBRR): An approach to early literacy instruction that is based on rigorous experimental research and focuses on explicit instruction on the skills and concepts that are the best predictors of later reading achievement.

formal assessment: Gathering information about learning during a special time set aside for testing.

informal assessment: Gathering information about learning while children engage in typical classroom activities.

Language Experience Approach: An approach to language learning in which students' oral compositions are transcribed and used as materials of instruction for reading, writing, speaking, and listening.

literacy-enriched play settings: Play centers that are enhanced with appropriate theme-related literacy materials such as recipe cards, cookbooks, and food containers for the kitchen center.

phonemic awareness: The awareness of the sounds (phonemes) that make up spoken words.

phonological awareness: Awareness of the constituent sounds of words in learning to read and spell.

shared reading: A classroom strategy in which a teacher reads a Big Book with enlarged print and encourages the children to read along on parts that they can remember or predict. Shared reading models the reading process and draws children's attention to print concepts and letter knowledge.

shared writing: A classroom strategy in which the teacher writes down children's own stories about their everyday experiences. These highly contextualized stories are easy for children to read.

specific indicators: Specific statements of what preschool children should know and be able to do.

standards: Statements that define what children should know and be able to do in a particular area such as literacy or mathematics.

writing center: A classroom area stocked with materials that invite children to engage in writing.

INTRODUCTION

Dee's Head Start classroom is hopping with excitement. The children and teachers are deeply involved in a unit on vehicles, a topic in which many children had expressed interest. Over the past several weeks, the class has made a field trip to a nearby mechanic's garage and has been visited by a fire engine crew, complete with hook-and-ladder truck, and a taxi driver. During large-group time, the children sing transportation-related songs and poems, and Dee uses these texts to make the children aware of rhyme and alliteration. In addition, Dee does **shared reading** with Big Books, including *Ella Sarah Gets Dressed* (Chodos-Irvine, 2003), and informational books such as *Truck Song* (Siebert, 1984) and *Sylvia's Garage* (Lee, 2002). Before and during reading, Dee provides direct instruction on book-related vocabulary (e.g., *author*, *cover*), **concepts of print** (e.g., directionality), and perhaps a comprehension strategy (e.g., predicting). After reading, Dee leads a rich discussion of children's reactions to the book and helps the children plan a book-related response activity involving writing, art, drama, or music.

The vehicle unit has spilled over into other parts of the classroom and curriculum. The **dramatic play** center has been transformed into a gas station and mechanic's garage. The children have brought props from home, such as an auto-repair manual and a tire pressure gauge. In addition, one child has brought in a broken scooter to be repaired by the "mechanics" at the station. Dee has also supplied many theme-related literacy props such as a pencil and notepad for writing out work orders and a wall sign that lists the prices for various types of repairs. During play time, Dee works with small groups of students and makes a scrapbook in which children can dictate what they have learned about vehicles, including lists of new words connected to this topic. Dee also helps the children learn to recognize letters in these words that have become so important to the children. In addition, the children write about their discoveries in learning logs, revealing various levels of emergent writing, such as scribbles, letterlike forms, letter streams, and invented spelling.

In recent years, the field of early literacy has been thrust into the spotlight; it is receiving an extraordinary amount of attention. A flurry of studies are providing preschool teachers with a wealth of knowledge about early literacy development and instruction. The U.S. government is funding large-scale research studies and professional development programs that focus on promoting young children's school readiness in the areas of language and literacy. Through such initiatives as *Good Start, Grow Smart*, the U.S. government is encouraging states to develop early learning guidelines aligned with their K–12 academic **standards**; develop rigorous professional development programs that focus on evidence-based early reading instruction; and coordinate literacy instruction in Head Start, public school preschools, and other early childhood programs. In addition, recent Head Start reauthorization bills have mandated that Head Start programs implement early literacy standards and conduct yearly **assessments** to determine how well children are meeting those standards. The times certainly are changing in early childhood education, particularly in the areas of oral language and early literacy (reading and writing).

There is an upside and a downside to all this attention. On the one hand, a tremendous amount of resources is being funneled into the early literacy field. The resulting research is helping to grow the knowledge about early literacy development and effective instruction. This research tells preschool educators that if children acquire certain knowledge, skills, and dispositions during the preschool years, they are likely to become successful readers and writers in the elementary grades.

Observation of Dee's classroom reveals many newly discovered research-based strategies for promoting young children's acquisition of core literacy knowledge, skills, and dispositions. In developmentally appropriate ways, Dee is helping her young students develop oral vocabulary, **phonemic awareness**, alphabet recognition, and concepts of print—the skills and knowledge that have been shown to predict later success in reading and writing.

While these new initiatives provide rich resources to improve early literacy instruction, they also present some daunting challenges. Preschool teachers are experiencing mounting pressure to increase children's literacy development, raising concerns that drill-and-practice, worksheets, basal readers, and other types of instruction will be pushed down from the elementary grades to the preschool level. Many teachers of young children worry that academic instruction and extensive testing will replace play, art, music, storybook reading that focuses on enjoyment of literature, and other activities that educate the whole child and encourage self-initiated learning.

Preschool teachers must take advantage of the positive developments and make every effort to avoid the potential negative outcomes. A challenging task? Yes. Possible? Absolutely. Research has identified the core content that young children need to learn in order to be successful readers and writers and also has identified a number of developmentally appropriate strategies for teaching these core skills, such as interactive storybook reading, **literacy-enriched play centers**, and **shared writing**. There is no need to impose elementary-grade strategies on the preschool curriculum. A whole range of developmentally appropriate teaching strategies is available to help young children acquire the knowledge and skills that will get them off to a good start in learning to read and write.

In this book we seek to help preschool teachers (those who want to be preschool teachers and those who are) and administrators respond to the new challenges in early literacy by providing up-to-date information on a number of topics important to them and their young learners. We describe how young children learn to read and write, both at home and in school. Knowing the latest ideas about how children learn to read and write helps preschool teachers and administrators decide what to observe in children's development, what activities to use in the classroom, and how to encourage parents to support children's learning at home. Knowing the research that supports those ideas helps preschool teachers explain why they are teaching particular skills and using particular strategies in the classroom. Knowing this research helps preschool administrators support good teachers and offer professional development opportunities that will help all teachers become more effective and all children learn more.

Our goal in this book is to provide preschool teachers and administrators with the foundations—the core content and the best-practice teaching strategies—needed to provide their young learners with balanced, effective early literacy instruction. To help preschool teachers develop this kind of instruction, we provide ideas on how to

- read with young children;
- create a carefully planned, print-rich classroom environment;
- join children's play;
- plan a daily schedule that meets children's learning needs;
- help parents help their children learn; and
- link language and literacy standards with child assessment and with instruction.

To help preschool teachers and administrators picture what these suggested activities look like in a preschool classroom, we provide descriptions of several activities in use by outstanding early childhood teachers. We also pose questions to encourage preschool teachers and preschool teachers in training to think about their teaching or what they are observing. We challenge current preschool teachers to reflect on their teaching. We challenge preschool administrators to observe the classrooms in their center through these new lenses. And we challenge teacher education candidates who want to be preschool teachers to ensure that their future teaching reflects the evidence-based, developmentally appropriate ideas presented in this book.

CHAPTER 1

How Children Learn to Read and Write

Currently, there are two main perspectives on early reading and writing: **emergent literacy** and **evidence-based reading research**. In the sections that follow, we briefly review the key beliefs and the research base of each of these diverging views of early literacy development and teaching. Then we present our position that the two views need to be merged in order to provide well-balanced, effective early literacy instruction for young children. Finally, we highlight some strategies teachers might use to support young children's literacy development.

Emergent Literacy

During the 1980s and 1990s, *emergent literacy* (a term coined by Marie Clay in 1966) became the dominant theoretical perspective in the field of early reading and writing. According to this social constructivist view, literacy acquisition has much in common with oral language development. Children begin learning about reading and writing at a very early age by observing and interacting with adults and other children as they use literacy in everyday activities such as writing shopping lists and in special literacy-focused routines such as storybook reading. On the basis of these observations and activities, children construct their own concepts about the functions and structure of print and then try these in play (e.g., pretending to read a favorite book to a doll) and in everyday situations (e.g., recognizing a favorite brand of cereal at the supermarket). Young children test their beliefs about how written language works and, based on how others respond and the results they get, modify these beliefs and construct more sophisticated systems of reading and writing. For example, their attempts at writing often evolve from scribbles, to letterlike forms, to random streams of letters, and finally to increasingly elaborate systems of invented spelling (Sulzby, 1990). Eventually, with lots of meaningful opportunities to engage in meaningful literacy activities, large amounts of interaction with adults and peers, and some incidental instruction, children become conventional readers and writers.

The emergent literacy perspective is based on several strands of research. We will briefly review some key findings from these studies. For more specific information and research citations, we recommend that readers consult the integrative reviews published in Volumes II and III of the *Handbook of Reading Research* (Sulzby & Teale, 1991; Yaden, Rowe, & MacGillivray, 2000) or a comprehensive early childhood language arts textbook (Morrow, 2005; Vukelich, Christie, & Enz, 2002).

Several pioneering emergent literacy studies focused on early readers, children who came to kindergarten already able to read some words (Clark, 1976; Durkin, 1966). Results showed that many early readers were of average intelligence, contradicting the commonly assumed link between early reading and intellectual giftedness. Parental interviews revealed that these children shared several characteristics, including an early interest in print and writing. The parents also reported that they frequently read stories to their children and took the time to answer their children's questions about written language. The parents rarely, if ever, gave these early readers any direct reading or writing instruction. These findings suggested that home experiences had an important role in promoting early reading.

> Young children quickly discover that print is functional and can be used to get things done in everyday life.

Concepts of Print

Research on early readers, in turn, stimulated interest in what typical preschool-age children were learning about literacy. Many of these early studies focused on children's **concepts of print**. For example, researchers discovered that many 3-year-olds come to expect print to be meaningful. This understanding becomes evident when children point to words on signs, cereal boxes, or menus and ask, "What does that say?" Or, after making marks on a piece of paper, they ask, "What did I write?"

Research also revealed that young children quickly discover that print is functional and can be used to get things done in everyday life. For example, many 3-year-olds are familiar with the purposes of different types of print, such as store signs, restaurant menus, and name labels on presents. Young children's knowledge of the functional uses of literacy also is demonstrated during dramatic play. Researchers have reported numerous incidents of preschoolers engaging in a variety of functional literacy activities while engaging in dramatic play, including jotting down phone messages, writing checks to pay for purchases, looking up recipes in cookbooks, and making shopping lists.

Environmental Print

Other researchers studied young children's ability to recognize **environmental print**—print that occurs in real-life contexts. Results showed that many 3- and 4-year-olds can identify product labels (Colgate, Cheerios, Pepsi), restaurant signs (McDonald's, Pizza Hut), and street signs (STOP) (McGee, Lomax, & Head, 1988). Children often begin to recognize the letters of the alphabet at about the same time as they "read" environmental print. This ability varies considerably among children, with some children recognizing up to a third of the alphabet by age 3 and others not learning any letters until age 5. Children's own names and highly salient environmental print are often the source of initial letter learning. Marcia Baghban (1984), for example, describes how *K* (K-Mart), *M* (McDonald's), and *G* (Giti) were among the first letters recognized by her 2-year-old daughter, Giti.

Developmental Trends

Another strand of emergent literacy research focused on developmental trends in early forms of reading and writing. For example, Elizabeth Sulzby (1990) asked preschool children to write stories and then to read what they had written. Based on this research, Sulzby identified seven broad categories of early writing: (1) drawing as writing, (2) scribble writing, (3) letterlike units, (4) nonphonetic letter strings, (5) copying from environmental print, (6) invented spelling, and (7) conventional writing. Sulzby discovered that, while there is a general movement from less mature forms toward more conventional forms, children move back and forth across these types of writing when composing texts and often combine several different types in the same composition. Sulzby (1985) also found that children's storybook-reading behaviors appear to follow a developmental pattern, with their attention gradually shifting from the pictures to aspects of print. In addition, the intonation of children's voices when reading gradually shifts from sounding like they are telling an oral story to sounding like they are reading.

Home Environment

A fourth and final strand of emergent literacy research has focused on young children's home environments in an attempt to discover factors that promote early literacy learning. These studies have revealed four groups of home factors that are particularly important in getting children off to a good start in learning to read and write.

Access to Print and Books. Literacy learning is facilitated when young children have easy access to books and opportunities to see lots of print. For example, plentiful home supplies of children's books have been found to be associated with early reading and interest in literature. It is also beneficial when parents and other caregivers take children to libraries and bookstores.

Adult Demonstrations of Literacy Behavior. When children see their family members use print for various purposes—writing shopping lists, paying bills, looking up programs in *TV Guide*, and writing notes to each other—they begin to learn about the practical uses of written language and to understand why reading and writing are activities worth doing. If their parents happen to model reading for pleasure, so much the better.

Supportive Adults. Early readers tend to have parents or other caregivers who are very supportive of their early attempts at literacy. While these adults rarely attempt to directly teach children how to read and write, they do support literacy growth by doing such things as

- reading aloud storybooks frequently;
- answering children's questions about print;
- pointing out letters and words in the environment;
- providing easy access to print materials;
- providing children with a wide variety of experiences such as trips to stores, parks, and museums; and
- initiating functional literacy activities such as suggesting that a child write a letter to Grandma or help make a shopping list.

Storybook Reading. Research has consistently shown that parent–preschooler storybook reading is positively related to outcomes such as language growth, early literacy, and later reading achievement. Other studies have identified ways in which storybook reading facilitates literacy growth (Barrentine, 1996; Durkin, 1966; Holdaway, 1979; Snow & Ninio, 1986). These ways include

- building positive attitudes about books and reading,
- providing children with a model of skilled reading,
- creating a context in which parents can informally teach vocabulary and concepts and provide support for children's early attempts at reading, and

• encouraging independent engagements with literacy by familiarizing children with stories and encouraging them to attempt to read the stories on their own.

Early childhood language arts programs based on the emergent literacy perspective feature experiences that are similar to those that children have in enriched home environments—print-rich settings, storybook reading, demonstrations of various forms of literacy, and many opportunities for children to engage in meaningful reading and writing activities. These types of emergent literacy experiences build on what children have already learned about written language, provide a smooth transition between home and school, and promote initial success with learning to read and write.

Shared Writing: An Emergent Literacy Strategy

Shared writing, also referred to as the **Language Experience Approach**, involves having children read texts composed of their own oral language. A child first dictates a story about a personal experience, and the teacher writes it down. The teacher reads the story back to the child and then gives him or her the opportunity to read it. This can be done with groups of children using the chalkboard or chart paper, or with individuals using regular writing paper.

Shared writing is an excellent way for teachers to demonstrate the relationship between oral and written language. It helps children to realize that what they say can be written down in print and that print can be read back as oral language.

Shared writing also presents opportunities for teachers to demonstrate the structure and conventions of written language. The children watch as the teacher spells words conventionally, leaves spaces between words, uses a left-to-right and top-to-bottom sequence, starts sentences and names with capital letters, and ends sentences with periods or other terminal punctuation marks. Through these demonstrations, children can see how the mechanical aspects of writing work.

The shared writing strategy has the additional advantage of making conventional writing and reading easier for children. By acting as scribe, the teacher removes mechanical barriers to written composition. The children's compositions are limited only by their oral language and experiential backgrounds. Reading is also made much easier because Language Experience stories are composed of the children's own oral language and based on their personal experiences. This close personal connection with the story makes it easy for children to predict the identity of unknown words in the text.

The following is a Language Experience story dictated by 5-year-old Eric after his class had been to see the puppet show *Pinocchio*.

> The girl was being silly. The manager was being the fox and the little silly girl was being the cat and was being silly meowing and trying to scratch Pinocchio. Then Pinocchio promised his dad he would go to school, but he didn't. And the silly girl and Pinocchio lied, and both their noses grew long, and then they both turned into donkeys.

When Eric read his story for the first time, he had to be prompted on only three words—*manager, scratch,* and *promised*. He was able to figure out many difficult words (e.g., *meowing* and *donkey*) from the story context. It is highly unlikely that he would have been able to recognize these words in an adult-authored text.

Note how the content of the story reflects what was personally meaningful to Eric. He was more interested in the antics of the "silly girl," a volunteer from the audience, than in the main plot of the Pinocchio story. The fact that Eric was reading *his own story* made up of *his own oral language* ensured a successful reading experience. This emphasis on personal meaning is a hallmark of emergent literacy teaching strategies.

Evidence-Based Reading Research

During the late 1980s and the 1990s, when the emergent literacy perspective was the prevailing view in early childhood education, another very different view of beginning literacy was gaining momentum, primarily in the fields of educational psychology and special education. This movement, commonly referred to as evidence-based reading research (EBRR), asserts that rigorous experimental research can reveal (a) the skills and concepts that young children need to master to become proficient readers and writers and (b) the most effective strategies for teaching this content.

Whereas emergent literacy has relied primarily on qualitative forms for research, the EBRR perspective uses well-designed correlational studies and tightly controlled, quantitative experiments, hence the label *evicence-based*. And while emergent literacy advocates place heavy value on the social and meaning-based aspects of literacy, EBRR has focused more on visual and auditory processing aspects of literacy (Rayner, Foorman,

Perfetti, Pesetsky, & Seidenberg, 2002). Reading for understanding is still the ultimate objective of instruction, but EBRR advocates believe that children must first master the skills that enable them to process print before comprehension becomes possible.

The EBRR perspective came into prominence with the landmark book *Beginning to Read: Thinking and Learning About Print* (Adams, 1990) and gained additional momentum with the publication of the National Research Council's book *Preventing Reading Difficulties in Young Children* (Snow, Burns, & Griffin, 1998). More recently, the evidence-based perspective has been used as the foundation for many U.S. Department of Education initiatives, including *Good Start, Grow Smart* and the *Early Reading First* and *Early Childhood Professional Development* grant programs. Each of these initiatives is a component of a federal early childhood policy aimed at helping states and local communities strengthen young children's early language and literacy learning.

> The EBRR movement has identified the core knowledge and skills young children must develop to become successful readers.

Perhaps the most valuable contribution of the EBRR movement is that it has identified the core knowledge and skills young children must develop to become successful readers. Longitudinal studies have shown that preschool-age children's *oral language* (expressive and receptive language, including vocabulary development), **phonological awareness**, and *alphabet knowledge* are predictive of reading achievement in the elementary grades (Snow et al., 1998). *Print awareness*, which includes concepts of print (e.g., understanding how print can be used) and conventions of print (e.g., left-to-right, top-to-bottom sequence), has been found to be positively correlated with reading ability in the primary grades. Print awareness has received considerable attention from emergent literacy researchers.

EBRR investigators have also focused on identifying effective strategies for teaching this core literacy content to young children. One of the most consistent research findings is that young children's phonological awareness and alphabet knowledge can be increased via explicit instruction. This instruction often takes the form of games and other engaging activities, but it also contains teacher modeling, guided practice, and independent practice.

Phonemic Awareness Instruction: An EBRR Strategy

EBRR has made several important contributions to the field of early literacy, including identifying key knowledge and skills that young children need to learn in order to be successful in learning to read. In addition,

EBRR has identified developmental sequences for some of these skills and effective direct instruction teaching strategies.

Phonemic awareness—children's awareness of the individual sounds that make up spoken words—is a good example. Research has shown that phonemic awareness in kindergarten is a strong predictor of future reading achievement (Snow et al., 1998) and that direct instruction in phonemic awareness exerts strong positive effects on reading and spelling development (National Institute of Child Health and Human Development [NICHD], 2000). In addition, researchers have also identified a developmental sequence that can help guide this instruction. Before young children can become aware of phonemes, they first must master phonological awareness and learn to recognize larger units of oral language, including words and syllables (Adams, 1990). Once they have mastered the understanding that speech is composed of words and syllables, they can then begin to develop phonemic awareness, including the ability to analyze, synthesize, and manipulate the phonemes that make up words.

Research suggests a sequence of instructional activities that starts by building the broader concepts of phonological awareness and then moves toward awareness and manipulation of phonemes (Adams, Foorman, Lundberg, & Beeler, 1998).

Listening.   These activities sharpen the children's ability to attend to sounds in general. For example, the teacher can place objects that make noise into a bag and invite a child to remove an object and demonstrate its sound (e.g., shake a rattle). The rest of the children close their eyes and try to guess the identity of the object making the sound (Ericson & Juliebö, 1998).

Rhyming.   These activities focus children's attention on the ending sounds of words. For example, children recite or sing well-known nursery rhymes such as "Jack and Jill." Once children are familiar with a rhyme, the teacher repeats it, leaving out a rhyming word, and asks the children to guess the missing rhyming words (*Jack and Jill went up a ___*) (Ericson & Juliebö, 1998).

Words and Sentences.   These activities develop children's awareness that language is made up of strings of words. For example, the teacher can have children clap the words in familiar nursery rhymes: *Jack* (clap) *and* (clap) *Jill* (clap) *went* (clap) *up* (clap) *a* (clap) *hill* (clap).

Awareness of Syllables.   These activities develop children's ability to analyze words into separate syllables and to combine syllables into words. For example, the teacher can help children tap out the syllables in each child's first name: *Ann* (tap), *Joe* (tap), *Su-zy* (tap, tap), *Jua-ni-ta* (tap, tap, tap). After each name has been tapped, the teacher can ask the children how many syllables they heard.

Sound Matching.   These activities ask children to decide which of several words begins with a specific sound. For example, the teacher shows children several pictures of familiar objects (dog, horse, elephant) and asks which begins with the /d/ sound.

Initial and Final Sounds.   In these activities, children are given words and asked to tell which sound occurs at the beginning or end. For example, the children are asked, "What's the sound that starts these words: *run, rabbit, roar*?"

Blending.   In these activities, children are asked to combine individual sounds to form words. For example, the teacher can tell the class that she is thinking of a small animal. Then she says the name of the animal in separate phonemes (/k/-/a/-/t/) and asks the class to guess the identity of the animal. This requires children to blend individual phonemes to produce the name of the animal (Yopp, 1992).

Segmentation.   This is the opposite of blending. Here, the teacher asks children to break up words into individual sounds (*cat* becomes /k//a//t/). Lucy Calkins (1996) calls the ability to segment words "rubber-banding," stretching words to hear the individual phonemes.

Phonemic Manipulation.   This more difficult phonemic awareness task requires children to mentally add, delete, substitute, or reverse phonemes in words. For example, the teacher can ask children to say a word and then say it again without the initial sound (*pant-ant, fog-og*) or build words by substituting onsets and rimes (*j-et, m-et, l-et, p-et*).

   A direct instruction approach can be used with these activities—the teacher models how to do the activity, provides guided practice, and finally presents opportunities for independent practice. For example, during large-group time, the teacher can demonstrate how to clap the syllables in a name. Then the children take turns clapping the syllables in their names, with help from the teacher. Finally, children can pick a partner and practice clapping syllables in their names and their friends' names on their own.

EBRR researchers have also recommended a number of other evidence-based teaching ideas such as

- engaging children in extended discussions and exposing them to rare words,
- print-rich classroom environments,
- interactive storybook-reading techniques such as **dialogic reading,** and
- **literacy-enriched play centers.**

(See Neuman, 2002, for a concise review of these ideas.)

Balanced Early Literacy Instruction

Our position on these two perspectives on early reading and writing is quite simple: We believe that the two perspectives need to be interwoven in order to provide young children with balanced, effective early literacy instruction. Both views make significant contributions to a well-rounded early literacy program. Children need meaningful, social engagements with books, various forms of print, and writing. In addition, most children also need some direct, developmentally appropriate instruction on phonological awareness, letter recognition, and vocabulary.

By combining the emergent literacy and EBRR perspectives, we have developed eight basic principles of effective early literacy instruction.

1. *Early language and literacy education should focus on core content—the knowledge, skills, and dispositions that are predictive of later success in learning to read and write.* This core content includes oral language, background knowledge, phonological awareness, alphabet knowledge, and concepts of print. Focusing on this core content will ensure that instructional time is being used optimally to promote children's academic readiness.

2. *Oral language lays the foundation for early literacy development.* Teachers should engage children in rich conversations and expose them to rare words that are not encountered in everyday speech. For instance, when studying transportation, children can be introduced to the names of different vehicles (e.g., pickup trucks, oil tankers, and airplanes), transportation occupations (e.g., taxi driver, truck driver, and mechanic), and transportation-related tools (e.g., tire pressure gauge, hydraulic lift).

When such key words are incorporated into daily activities, children come to know their meanings.

3. *Storybook reading is the cornerstone of early literacy instruction.* Children need to be read to frequently—in large groups and small groups, with little books and Big Books, and using a variety of texts, including storybooks, informational books, and poetry. Children should actively engage in these reading sessions, making predictions, asking questions, offering their reactions and opinions, and having opportunities to participate in book-related activities.

4. *A carefully planned classroom environment enables literacy development to flourish.* Teachers should provide children with a print-rich classroom environment that will encourage children to engage in emergent forms of reading and writing. There should be a well-stocked library center, a writing center, many examples of functional print, and literacy-enriched play settings. In addition, the day should be scheduled with sensitivity to young children's learning and developmental needs, providing large blocks of time for individual and small-group activities and shorter amounts of time for whole-group, teacher-led activities.

5. *Children need opportunities to engage in emergent forms of reading and writing.* Children should be presented with meaningful opportunities to engage in reading and writing. They should have opportunities to investigate the books that are read during storybook-reading sessions and to engage in functional reading (e.g., attendance lists, calendars, daily schedules) and writing activities (e.g., sign-up sheets for popular learning centers). There also should be opportunities for them to incorporate literacy into their play activities.

6. *Developmentally appropriate forms of direct instruction should be used to teach core literacy concepts and skills.* Teachers can teach many concepts of print while engaging children in **shared reading**. For example, they can use a pointer to model the left-to-right and top-to-bottom sequence of written language and then invite children to use the pointer—first with some support, and later on their own with a partner. Rhymes, songs, and games can be used to teach important phonological awareness skills.

7. *Teachers need to help parents support their children's language, reading, and writing development.* Many parents and other primary caregivers underestimate the importance of their role in helping their children become competent language users and successful readers. Teachers must discover ways to work with their students' parents in order to ensure the development of confident readers and writers. Given the variety of family

structures today, "parent" must be broadly defined. In some families, the "parent" may be an older sibling, or a grandparent, or foster parents, or two moms. The key is for the teacher to connect with the people who are significant in each child's life.

8. *Oral language and early literacy instruction and **assessment** should be guided by **standards** that define the knowledge and skills young children need to become successful readers and writers.* Many U.S. states have recently adopted oral language and early literacy standards for prekindergarten students. These research-based guidelines define what children in that state should know and be able to do before entering kindergarten. Teachers must be aware of their state's standards and must use them as guides in planning their daily instruction and in assessing their student's learning.

Here we see how the core EBRR teaching strategy, dialogic reading, can be infused with elements from the emergent literacy perspective.

Interactive Storybook Reading: A Blended Strategy

Dialogic reading is based on the assumption that *how* teachers read to children is as important as *how often* teachers read to children. The Stony Brook Reading and Language Project developed the dialogic reading strategy in order to help adults read to young children in a way that involves the children in the reading process (Whitehurst, 1992). In dialogic reading, the adult helps the child become the storyteller. The adult, instead of the child, is the listener. Children whose teachers use this method make greater gains on tests of their language development than children of teachers who do not (Arnold & Whitehurst, 1994).

This is how dialogic reading works. Think PEER:

P The adult *prompts* the child to say something about the book.

E The adult *evaluates* the child's response.

E The adult *expands* on the child's response by rephrasing and adding information to the child's response.

R The adult *repeats* the prompt to make sure that the child has learned from the expansion.

What does this sound like in an adult–child storybook reading? Take a look into a preschool classroom and see the PEER approach in action.

A teacher is getting ready to share *Brown Bear, Brown Bear, What Do You See?* (Martin, 1992) with his students. He begins by holding up the front of the book for the children to see, pointing to the animal on the cover, and asking, "What is this?" This is the prompt. A child says, "It's a bear." The teacher responds, "That's right (*evaluation*); it's a brown bear (*expansion*). Can you all say *brown bear*?" (*repetition*). Then the teacher points to the words on the cover of the book and reads the title and the names of the author and illustrator. He invites the children to read the words with him.

The reading of the print, with the children's help, is our addition to the PEER procedure. We have blended a core EBRR procedure, dialogic reading, with the shared reading strategy from the emergent literacy perspective.

To further help adults, the Stony Brook Reading Project developed a list of types of prompts adults might use. Think CROWD:

C *Completion prompts*: Leave a blank at the end of the sentence and ask the children to fill it in. "Brown Bear, Brown Bear, What do you see? I see a red bird looking at _____." Completion prompts help children learn about the structure of language.

R *Recall prompts*: These kinds of prompts are questions about the story's plot, sequence of events, or characters. Questions such as "What did the children see looking at them?" help children focus on their understanding of the story.

O *Open-ended prompts*: Prompts like "Tell me about what you see happening in this picture" encourage children to attend to details.

W *What, where, when, why, and how questions*: These prompts are intended to teach vocabulary. The teacher might point to each of the animals in the book and ask the children to name each one.

D *Distancing prompts*: These kinds of prompts ask the children to relate what was read to events outside the book, for example, "Remember the brown bear we saw at the zoo?" Distancing prompts link the book's text and the children's experiences.

By engaging in these kinds of activities while reading with children, teachers show children how to make sense of the text and how to construct meaning while listening to or reading books. By prompting and encouraging the children to talk (to ask questions, respond to others' questions, and notice the illustrations and the print), the teacher is helping the children understand how readers construct the meaning of a text as the story or information unfolds. Through these activities, teachers can engage their young learners with print.

In the remaining chapters, we will pay particular attention to two principles: (1) Classroom environments can be a powerful catalyst to literacy learning (see chapter 2), and (2) home–school connections are critical to children's literacy development (see chapter 4).

Creating a Literacy-Rich Environment for Young Children

Think about the preschool classroom that you know best. Does it look like the classroom in Figure 1 or Figure 2? What are the differences between these two classrooms? One of the two has the appearance of a classroom designed to support children's learning. Which one? Why?

If you selected Figure 2 as the better-designed preschool classroom, congratulations! The teacher who created this classroom environment used the principles we will discuss in this chapter to create a quality place for young children to play and learn.

Arranging the Classroom

Divide the large classroom space into small centers. In designing a learning environment for young children, bigger is not always better. When young children enter a learning center, they first explore and examine the materials. Exploration is followed by more complex, meaningful play. Small, well-defined spaces encourage children to focus on the materials at hand, interact with other children, and persist in their play activities. Research has shown that when the space is snug but not cramped, with room enough for five or six children, children's play becomes more complex and more meaningful, and their play lasts for a longer time (DeLong et al., 1994).

Use movable furniture to create defined play spaces or centers. Classroom furniture such as bookshelves and tables can serve as dividers to define the play centers. Chart stands, puppet stages, artificial trees, and housekeeping props, such as wooden ovens and refrigerators, can also serve this purpose. When the boundaries of each play area are marked clearly, children discover how to use the play space more effectively.

Arrange the furniture within each center to encourage the children to interact with one another. Children can learn from one another as they play in each center. To encourage children to play together, Myae Han and James Christie (2001) advise teachers to group the chairs to facilitate

Figure 1
An Open Classroom Space

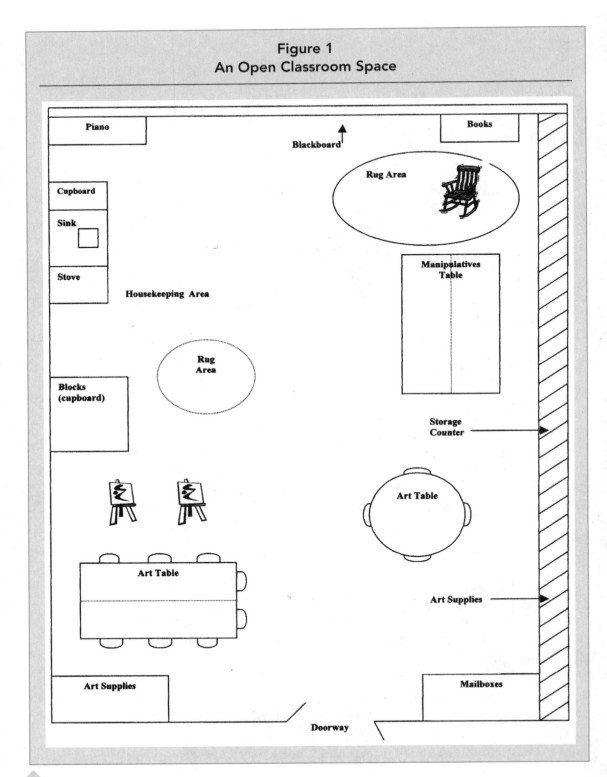

Figure 2
Classroom Space Divided Into Centers

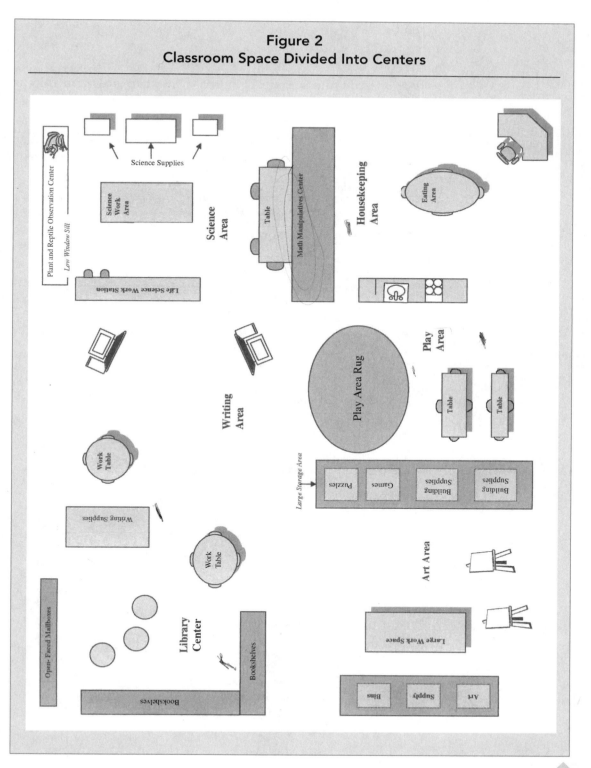

conversation and to provide multiple sets of props. Placing pairs of chairs in front of classroom computers encourages children to collaborate while using the computer to play games, get information, and write texts.

Place related centers near each other. If the **writing center** is next to the library center, children will be encouraged to write about the books they are reading. The science center should be near the mathematics center, and the block center near the housekeeping center. Placing similar centers near each other encourages children to use a variety of materials to support their explorations.

Some features of the classroom in Figure 2 cannot be seen from an aerial perspective. Looking directly into a center makes other important features visible. Notice how, in Figure 3, the teacher has used print to define

Figure 3
The Writing Center

the types of activities that should occur in the area. First, the teacher used a sign to label the center. She thought a great deal about what to name the center because it is important to use labels that children will understand. For example, teachers might label the **dramatic play** center Housekeeping Center, Dress-Up Corner, or Home Corner. Such labels help define the purpose of the center for the children. The Housekeeping Area is a place for children to play what they see happening in their home. The Dress-Up Corner is a place to wear dress-up clothes. Similarly, teachers might label the library center Book Corner or Reading Corner. Prior to coming to preschool, some young children will have little or no experience with libraries. Using a label like Book Corner makes it clear that this center is a place for reading books.

Next, the teacher hung the sign low, at the children's eye level, and put pictures next to the label. A picture helps the children "read" the print and gives purpose for their play in the area. Such strategies gently coax the children to engage in behaviors appropriate to the center's activity.

The teacher also added functional signs to the center. "Write books here" encourages the children to use the small blank books to write their stories and "Open" indicates that the center is available for play today.

Finally, the teacher labeled the materials storage places and added a picture next to the print. These labels, with pictures, help the children to find the needed materials and to return the used materials to their appropriate places—making clean-up time much easier for the teacher and the children. Notice also how similar materials (paper, writing tools) are grouped together to help the children see categories of materials.

Another way to enrich the classroom literacy environment is to bring in lots of **environmental print** that children see in their lives outside the classroom—print such as *STOP*, *McDonald's*, and *Cheerios*. Many young children learn to "read" this kind of print through their many experiences with it. The research on children's reading of environmental print suggests that children use context to help them read the word. That is, at the grocery store, they point and demand, "I want that one—Cheerios!" They seem able to read the word *Cheerios*. However, when *Cheerios* is cut off the box and the picture is removed, children no longer can read the word; they need the whole cereal box in full color with the picture to read *Cheerios*. By themselves, experiences with environmental print do not result in children learning to read. However, learning to read environmental print does help children learn to expect print to have meaning and to know that groups of letters make up something that can be read. When teachers add labels to the classroom environment and point them out as part of the daily routine, children's knowledge of print grows. Classroom labels become as familiar and meaningful as the logos and street signs found throughout the community. Consider the experience of 4-year-old Andre.

● ● ● ● ● ● ● ● ● ● ● ● ● ● ● ●

Andre waits by the classroom door for his friends to join him. He looks up at the "Exit" sign above the door. He turns to his teacher and says, "I know what that says: Go outside." (He makes *outside* two words, *out* and *side*.) As he says each word, he points to a letter. But one letter remains. He corrects himself. "Oh no, it says: Go out side here."

● ● ● ● ● ● ● ● ● ● ● ● ● ● ● ●

Designing Learning Centers

Ecological psychologists have researched the importance of the environment on children's learning. A conclusion from these researchers' work is that children's behavior is greatly influenced by the classroom environment. Teachers who want children to behave like readers and writers must create a classroom environment that coaxes young children into being readers and writers. What might such an environment look like? It should contain two key centers—a library center with lots of books and an environment that encourages reading, and a writing center that contains materials and resources for writing. In addition to these core literacy centers, teachers should put materials to support children's reading and writing explorations in every area in the classroom.

The Library Center

Did you know that in many early childhood classrooms, books are not present in the quantity, quality, or variety that young children deserve and need to support their learning? In fact, some early childhood classrooms do not even have a library center.

Take a look at Figure 4. This is the kind of well-designed library center that every young learner needs and deserves. Five or six children can fit into this area. Remember, the goal is to create a space that is snug but not cramped. Here, small groups of children can gather to read, write, talk, and listen. Note that the center is labeled, and there is a picture next to the sign showing appropriate center behavior to help the children read the label. Writing tools and blank booklets enable children to record their own sto-

Figure 4
The Library Center

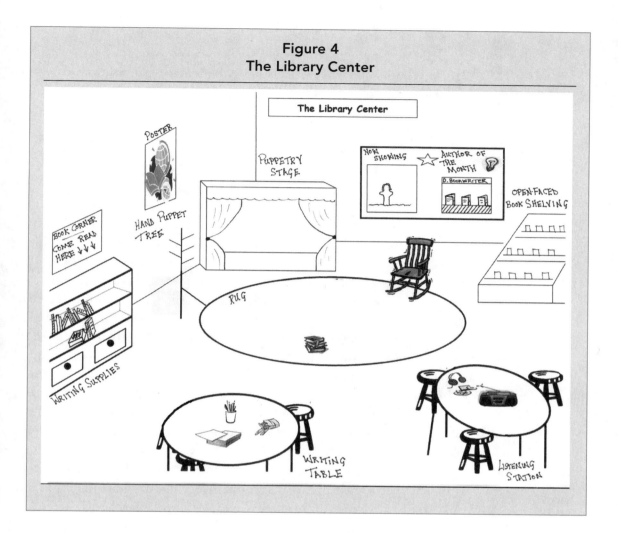

ries. With a bit of imagination and planning, the library center can become one of the most inviting areas of the classroom. Take a look at this innovative library center.

• • • • • • • • • • • • • • •

Each classroom in St. Michael's Day Nursery has a brightly colored, painted claw-foot tub filled with pillows. The tubs were gifts of a building demolition contractor. He and a work crew delivered them to the designated spot in each classroom. Two local AmeriCorps VISTA members, as a part of their service commitment, painted the tubs—one red, one blue, one green, one yellow. Colorful pillows from rummage sales, thrift stores, and homes fill the bottom of each tub. One group of children insisted that all the pillows be blue, like water.

Three rules apply to the reading tubs. These rules are posted above each tub, with picture support.

1. Maximum of two children in the tub at one time.

2. Shoes off.

3. Read.

● ● ● ● ● ● ● ● ● ● ● ● ● ● ● ●

Open-faced and traditional bookshelves provide children with easy access to books. The books on the traditional bookshelf are shelved with their spines out. These types of shelves have the advantage of being able to store lots of books. The open-faced bookshelf does not hold many books, but it allows the children to see each book's cover. Children will choose more books from the open-faced bookshelf than from the traditional bookshelf. Researchers found that when both types of shelves were used, kindergartners chose more than 90% of their books from open-faced shelves (Fractor, Woodruff, Martinez, & Teale, 1993). Some teachers put all the books about the current topic of study into a special bin. During Time to Read and Activity Time, the children are free to select books from this special collection as well as books from the bookshelves.

If an open-faced bookshelf is too expensive for a center's budget, Linda Gambrell (2000) suggests teachers make a book rail. A book rail accomplishes the same function as an open-faced bookshelf—it displays books so that children can see the covers. The only difference is that, instead of being free-standing, it is attached to a wall. Here is how Gambrell suggests that teachers make their own book rail:

1. Go to a home repair store.

2. Purchase a piece of aluminum drain gutter.

3. Back in the classroom, rest the gutter against the wall (or attach it to the wall at eye level, if this is permitted), and put books facing out into the slot.

Goal: To catch readers!

Numerous props, such as puppets, stuffed animals, and a flannelboard with storybook characters are available for the children's use. Children might decide to read a book to a teddy bear or retell a story using hand puppets or flannelboard characters, or they might collect three bears and retell the story of the three little bears with friends.

Book-related displays including an author bulletin board attract children to the center. Inexpensive posters to brighten the center and encourage reading can be obtained from the Children's Book Council and the American Library Association. Also, the exhibit halls at regional and national teacher and library conferences are excellent sources for free children's book posters.

The better the design of the library center, the more the children use it. Does the library center in the preschool classroom you know best look like Figure 4? What about the books in the library center? What materials are needed to support children's literacy learning? If there are 15 children in a preschool classroom, how many books should be in the library center? Lesley Morrow (2005) recommends that a classroom library should contain five to eight books per child. That means that a classroom with 15 children needs 75 to 120 books. Building a collection of this size need not be expensive.

Building a Classroom Library.   Following are some inexpensive ways to build a classroom library:

- Invite a local club to adopt your classroom. Ask the club to contact members for picture books and children's magazine donations.
- Visit area flea markets, rummage sales, and thrift stores. Get to know the clerks. Perhaps they'll call when picture books are donated.
- Make friends with your local public library's children's librarian. Arrange to borrow as many books as possible each month. Here you will find a ready source of books linked to the topic being studied in the classroom. If the public library is within walking distance, arrange to take the children to the library to introduce them to the wonders available there.
- Organize a fundraiser to purchase books for the classroom.
- Invite parents to give a book to the classroom in honor of their child's birthday.
- Join a paperback book club and use the bonus points to purchase books.

Some of the 75 to 120 books in the classroom library center need to remain in the center for the entire year. These are the core books that children continuously read and reread. These are the books whose titles the children shout when asked, "What would you like me to read to you today?" Other books will rotate in and out of the center. Often, these books are linked with the topic the children are studying. Studying transportation? Gather books about cars, trucks, taxis, and airplanes from your local library. Studying food? The library center needs both fiction and informational books on different foods.

Selecting Books for the Classroom Library.   What kinds of books belong in a preschool classroom library? Strive to provide quality literature on a variety of topics. Following are a few recommendations, including longstanding favorites and some newer titles.

- Traditional stories such as *Goldilocks and the Three Bears* (Aylesworth, 2003) and *Just a Minute: A Trickster Tale and Counting Book* (Morales, 2003)

- Picture books with rich language, varied sentence structure, and sophisticated vocabulary, such as *My Family Plays Music* (Cox, 2003), *My Name Is Yoon* (Recorvits, 2003), and *My Friend Rabbit* (Rohmann, 2002)

- Classic storybooks by authors such as Tomie dePaola, Eric Carle, Paul Galdone, Tana Hoban, Ezra Jack Keats, Leo Lionni, and Robert McCloskey

- Poetry including *¡Pío Peep! Traditional Spanish Nursery Rhymes* (Flor & Campoy, 2003), *Honey I Love* (Greenfield, 1978), *Up the Hill and Down* (Smith, 2003), *Best Mother Goose Ever!* (Scarry, 1999), and *Will Moses' Mother Goose* (Moses, 2003)

- Alphabet books such as *The Animal ABC* (Baker, 2003), *ABC: A Child's First Alphabet Book* (Jay, 2003), and *Alphabeep: A Zipping, Zooming ABC* (Pearson, 2003)

- Predictable stories such as *Brown Bear, Brown Bear, What Do You See?* (Martin, 1992), *Chicka Chicka Boom Boom* (Martin & Archambault, 1989), *Chicken Soup With Rice* (Sendak, 1962), *Ella Sarah Gets Dressed* (Chodos-Irvine, 2003), *I Kissed the Baby* (Murphy, 2003), and *Hi, Harry* (Waddell, 2003)

- Informational or expository texts such as *Truck* (Crews, 1997), *Tool Book* (Gibbons, 1988), *The Quicksand Book* (dePaola, 1977), *What Do You Do With a Tail Like This?* (Jenkins & Page, 2003), *What Is an Artist?* (Lehn, 2002), and *I Face the Wind* (Cobb, 2003)

Young children are very curious about how their world works. Therefore, including nonfiction books in the library center is critically important. Yet, Nell Duke's (2000) study of young children's classrooms found very few informational books. What kinds of books are in the preschool classroom you know best? How many books of each kind are available for the children's use in this classroom? What about children's magazines? These, too, should be found in the library center.

The Writing Center

Some teachers put the writing center in a section of the library center. They put a table, chairs, writing tools, and small blank books in the library center to encourage children to write books. Others set up a writing center adjacent to the library center with lots of different kinds of paper and writing tools for children's use.

In the writing center, teachers can also provide models of different types of writing, including invitations, greeting cards, postcards, letters, and thank-you notes, for the children to use as a resource for writing. Another important resource is alphabet strips, laid flat on the table so children can hunt for and copy the letters they need. Often, children will write using their personal script, ignoring the alphabet strip—they are, after all, preschool children. Teachers should also stock the writing center with materials that invite children to write and to play with writing. Consider the following possibilities:

- Assorted paper, such as unlined paper, envelopes, notecards, story paper, paper cut into different shapes, and discarded office paper with one clean side
- An assortment of writing tools such as pencils, markers, crayons, felt-tip pens, and a computer
- Mailboxes for everyone in the class
- Writing folders
- A file cabinet or a box (a pizza box works well) to house the children's "works in progress"
- A bulletin board for displaying writing samples and children's writing efforts
- Posters of people engaged in writing
- Wooden or magnetic alphabet letters
- Clipboards

Such enticing materials coax young children into becoming writers. Labeled storage areas enable children to participate in clean-up.

Should computers be included in the writing center? Definitely yes! Some fortunate young children have access to computers at home. The language of computers is a natural part of their vocabulary, and they are accustomed to using computers to support their learning. But all preschoolers need such opportunities. Otherwise, the digital divide will persist and inevitably some children will miss the chance to learn with this valuable resource. A computer in the classroom is a tool, just like a pencil or a book. Put books and writing implements in the classroom, and they become a part of the children's lives. Put computers in the classroom, and the same thing happens. Computers become tools for literacy play, as we see in the following exchange.

● ● ● ● ● ● ● ● ● ● ● ● ● ● ● ●

Angie finds 3-year-old Lauren sitting at the keyboard, tapping the computer keys. Cautiously, she asks, "What are you doing, Lauren?" Lauren turns and says, "Checkin' my e-mail."

● ● ● ● ● ● ● ● ● ● ● ● ● ● ● ●

New software packages appear on the market each year. Some current favorites include Orly's Draw-a-Story and Claris for Kids. For some preschool classrooms, computers are an expensive tool. To stretch the budget as far as possible, contact a local business (e.g., a bank or university) to learn about the possibility of securing their "gently used" computers and printers for free. Then, technology funds can be used to purchase the software and Internet access needed to make the computers useful to the children.

Putting the Tools for Reading and Writing Throughout the Classroom

Having books and writing tools in the library center and writing center is not enough. Print and tools to make print need to be placed in every classroom center—dramatic play, art, science, math, and so forth. When reading and writing are part of every activity, young children have many opportunities to learn, practice, and consolidate literacy concepts and skills. By embedding reading and writing materials into dramatic play centers, teachers provide children with opportunities to do what Jerome

Bruner (1984) calls "run ups" to literacy. Through their play in these **literacy-enriched play settings**, children can practice being readers and writers. They get to try on the role of taxi driver, garage worker, doctor, or architect and to use the tools of literacy connected with each role. They provide receipts for rides given or car repairs made. They read the stop signs as they drive their customers to their destination. They read and follow the directions for changing a tire. They write prescriptions. They read magazines while they wait for their doctor's appointment. They make architectural drawings before they build, labeling the parts of the building.

> The most complex forms of language appear first in children's play.

Of course, this literacy-enrichment strategy is not restricted to the literacy centers. If pencils and markers are placed in the art center, children will have opportunities to write their names on creations. With some guidance from the teacher, they also will begin to write signs (e.g., "Ples dnt tch") to protect art projects in progress. If markers and sign-making materials are placed in the block center, children will make safety signs to go along with their constructions. When pencils and notepads are available in the science center, children can jot down notes and observations. They can record when the fish have been fed or note how many baby fish are still alive.

Putting reading and writing materials in every center not only provides children with the opportunity to handle books, paper, and writing tools, but it also encourages them to use the vocabulary and sentence structures associated with each play setting. Bruner (1983) has noted that the most complex forms of language appear first in children's play activity. Possessing rich language skills is critical to children's later success as readers.

Creating Literacy-Enriched Play Settings

There is a powerful research base that supports the importance of teachers providing children with literacy-enriched play opportunities. Kathleen Roskos and James Christie (2001) studied the literacy-enriched play research and came to three conclusions:

1. Play provides a setting that promotes literacy activity, skills, and strategies.
2. Play serves as a language experience that can build connections between oral and written modes of expression.
3. Play provides opportunities for teachers to teach and children to learn literacy.

So, what might these play environments look like? What should teachers consider as they plan for children's play in literacy-enriched play settings?

First, a key principle:

Young children play best what they know. Therefore, literacy-enriched play settings should reflect real-life literacy situations (Neuman & Roskos, 1992). Teachers can support children in playing what they know—both by establishing play environments that relate to children's life experience and by providing classroom experiences that extend children's knowledge base.

Children come to school knowing something about family life. Common experiences include caring for a baby, shopping for groceries, cooking, and eating meals. Therefore, many preschool teachers set up a home play setting in the dramatic play center. These home play settings can be easily turned into literacy-enriched play environments by adding reading materials typical of a home, such as a telephone directory, books, television guides, newspapers and magazines, advertisements, cookbooks, and coupons, as well as writing materials such as pencils and notepads, sticky notes, stationery and envelopes, and checkbooks. When these materials are available for children's use in their play episodes, they will use them. The materials will nudge them to behave like readers and writers.

Near the housekeeping center, some teachers establish a theme setting based on the topic the children are studying. If space is limited, the housekeeping center can gradually be converted into a theme center, with new play props for each topic of study. For example, when studying food, the theme setting often is a restaurant. When studying transportation, the theme setting might be a garage, a taxi stand, a bus, or an airport terminal. By drawing from children's experiences at home, in school, and in the community, teachers can plan meaningful and productive settings. When studying health, the theme setting might be a doctor's office. Because most children have visited a pediatrician's office or health clinic, this is often an effective setting. Many children are fascinated by animals, and a veterinarian's office is another possibility—one that might add a new word to the children's vocabulary.

In setting up a theme center, it is essential to use furniture and props suggestive of real-world settings. For example, a veterinarian's office might be divided into a waiting area and an examination room. In the waiting area, patients might sit in chairs, while a receptionist sits behind a desk and jots down essential information. Literacy props in this area could include reading material for pet owners and a telephone book, message pad, appointment book, patient folders, and forms and clipboards for the receptionist. Wall signs such as "Exit," "Please Ring Bell for Service," and "The Doctor Is In" enhance the literacy environment.

Surrounding the examination table, literacy props might include a doctor's kit, a scale, and informational books and charts about pets. Given such materials, children will recall their own experiences at the doctor and will draw from their observations of adults engaged in medical roles. Because the tools needed by readers and writers are readily available to the children, the children will incorporate them into their play. They will sign the appointment book, fill out the required forms, answer the telephone, and take messages. They will behave like readers and writers, using the language associated with the roles they assume. For additional ideas on literacy materials that might be added to various thematic play settings, see Appendix A.

Such play settings provide children with a supportive context for meaningful, authentic interactions with reading and writing. While children play, they have the opportunity to practice learning about the purposes for print and about the conventions of writing and reading. And as they play, they begin to see reading and writing as something they want to be able to do. Thus, linking literacy and play builds print motivation—positive attitudes toward reading and writing that can have an important role in later literacy learning.

Children's writing during play may not be conventional print. In fact, it probably will not be. See Figure 5 for an example of scribble writing inspired by a supportive play setting.

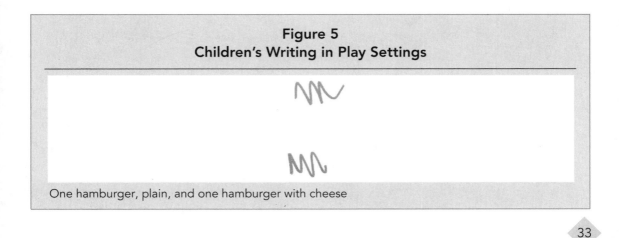

Figure 5
Children's Writing in Play Settings

One hamburger, plain, and one hamburger with cheese

Children come to understand that print has meaning. In the following classroom scene, notice how Kayla uses writing.

● ● ● ● ● ● ● ● ● ● ● ● ● ● ●

The play setting is a restaurant. Kayla, the waitress with an order pad and pencil in hand, approaches a table of customers with the questions, "What do ya want? Paghetti? Hamburger?" After considerable negotiating about what really is available from the menu and several conversations with the cook, the customers decide on spaghetti, one with meatballs and one without meatballs. Kayla writes the order, using scribblelike script. She tears the order from the pad and hands it to the cook saying, "Two orders of 'paghetti, one with meatballs and with none." The cook looks at the order and asks, "What did you write?" Kayla responds, "Paghetti with meatballs and paghetti with none! And hurry up! They are hungry!" The cook gets busy banging pots and cooking.

● ● ● ● ● ● ● ● ● ● ● ● ● ● ●

What does Kayla show us she knows? She demonstrated her awareness of the practical functions of print. To remember an order, she needed to write it down.

Signs such as "Please Wait to Be Seated" or "No Customers in the Kitchen" encourage children to ask, "What does that say?" They quickly understand that print has meaning—and they use that knowledge to control their peers' behavior. "You can't go in the kitchen. Only me!" Also, repeated exposure to print props gives children opportunities to recognize sight words. They begin to read *No, Exit, Open,* and *Closed*:

● ● ● ● ● ● ● ● ● ● ● ● ● ● ●

Jasmine and Tiki are playing together in the Shoe Store dramatic play center. When any other child approaches, one of them runs to the "Closed" sign and says, "What does this say? *Closed.* We'll tell you when we are open. You can't come in 'til then."

● ● ● ● ● ● ● ● ● ● ● ● ● ● ●

Some children begin to recognize letters through their repeated exposure to print during play. For example, they begin to recognize *O* because it is the first letter in *Open.* Other children might begin to learn about sound–symbol relationships. For example, if *pizza, pepperoni,* and *Pepsi* are on the menu in the restaurant play center, children may begin to discover that all these words start with the same sound and that this sound is represented by the letter *p.*

The Teacher's Role

It seems difficult to argue that writing materials and print are not important features of a quality play center. But still there is something missing—the teacher. With teacher involvement, children learn more about reading and writing than when they play alone or solely with other children. Billie Enz and James Christie (1997) describe three important roles that teachers can assume in children's play; each role is important to children's learning. First, teachers can be *stage managers*. As stage managers, they gather materials, make props, organize the play area, and talk with the children about how they might play in the setting. Second, teachers can also be *coplayers*. As coplayers, they join in the children's play and assume a minor role appropriate to the setting. For example, in a restaurant play setting, they might be customers. In this role, they might ask about the items on the menu, ask about paying with a credit card or with a check, help other customers place their orders, ask about a particular sign, and so forth.

> With teacher involvement, children learn more about reading and writing than when they play alone or solely with other children.

Through their behavior, they can model reading and writing behaviors associated with the role, like writing a check. Finally, teachers can be *play leaders*. As play leaders, teachers take steps to enrich and extend the play episodes. They introduce conflict into the play. For example, in a restaurant play setting as the customer, a teacher might order something that is not on the menu. When the child says that the requested food is not on the menu, the teacher might ask, "Isn't there anything you can do?" This creates a problem for the children to solve and enriches the play episode. If the children have no suggestions, the teacher might ask, "Could you go to the grocery store to get the ingredients?" If the children agree, then the teacher might question the children's ability to remember everything that is needed, by asking, "Is there anything that you could do to help you remember?" Perhaps the children will consider writing a grocery list. Teachers likely will play each of these roles regularly. The key is to watch the children at play and to choose the role that best fits the children's ongoing play episode.

When teachers act as stage managers and add reading and writing materials to all their classroom centers, they coax young children into engaging in reading and writing behaviors. When teachers go a step further and become coplayers and play leaders, they can provide children with meaningful reading and writing opportunities. Through such play, children practice the important reading and writing skills.

Evaluating the Classroom Environment

Creating a quality place for children to play and learn requires teachers to carefully plan the classroom environment. When you look at a preschool classroom, ask yourself the following questions:

Has the large classroom space been divided into small, well-defined areas?

Was the furniture arranged to encourage the children to interact with each other?

Are related centers near each other?

Is each learning center labeled with a sign? Are the signs displayed at children's eye level? Can the children understand the signs?

Are the storage places for materials labeled?

Is there functional and/or environmental print in each center?

Is there a library center with a generous selection of books? Are the books displayed on both open-faced and traditional bookshelves?

Is there a writing center that offers an assortment of appealing writing materials with and on which children can write for various purposes?

Does the dramatic play center contain theme-related reading and writing materials from the world outside the classroom?

Do the play settings build on the children's background knowledge?

Does the teacher enter the play settings to play with the children?

If you can answer *yes* to each of these questions, you know that you are observing a carefully planned, literacy-rich preschool learning environment.

CHAPTER 3

Planning the Daily Schedule

Young children need time to investigate on their own, in small groups with their peers and teachers, and in a large group. Although there is need for flexibility in the schedule so that children are allowed to pursue their interests without interruption, young children also need predictability. Children thrive when they know that the whole-group meeting is followed by activity time, that activity time is followed by snack time, and so forth.

The following principles enable preschool teachers to create a daily schedule that is sensitive to young children's learning and developmental needs.

- Quiet times should be balanced with noisier times, and sitting and listening time should be balanced with movement time.
- Large blocks of time for individual and small-group investigations should be balanced with shorter amounts of time for whole-group activities.
- Large blocks of time for children to make decisions should be balanced with shorter amounts of time during which the teacher leads activities.

What might a daily schedule that meets these criteria look like? Figure 6 provides an example of two preschool schedules, one for a half-day program and the other for a full-day program.

Must teachers follow a prescribed schedule every day? Carol Anne Wien and Susan Kirby-Smith (1998) say no. They suggest that teachers establish a predictable order for daily events and that they allow the children to dictate the timing of the changes in activities. They believe that what children need is predictability and a structure to each day, not a schedule determined by the clock. If the children are deeply engaged in investigations during activity time, what is wrong with extending their play another 5 to 10 minutes? On the other hand, if the children seem disengaged, if they are wandering the classroom and struggling with one

Figure 6
Daily Schedules

A Sample Half-Day Schedule

8:00–8:30	Children arrive, sign in, use library center materials while waiting for group time to begin
8:30–9:00	Whole-group morning gathering, morning messages, discussion of the topic being studied, overview of the day
9:00–10:00	Activity time in literacy-enriched play settings; teacher works with small groups of children on literacy activities suited to their needs
10:00–10:20	Clean-up and snack
10:20–10:45	Shared storybook reading (with lots of discussion)
10:45–11:15	Outdoor play
11:15–11:45	Songs, poems, movement
11:45–12:00	Review of the day and preparation for going home

A Sample Full-Day Schedule

The morning might proceed as above, with the exception of the review of the day at 11:45.

11:45–12:15	Lunch
12:15–12:40	Storybook reading in small groups
12:40–1:40	Rest (children may not actually sleep)
1:40–2:40	Outdoor play
2:40–3:10	Math-related activities
3:10–4:10	Activity/play time in literacy-enriched play settings; teacher works with small groups of children on literacy activities suited to their needs
4:10–4:40	Whole-group circle time that focuses on summarizing the day's activities, predicts tomorrow's activities, and reviews stories read in group times
4:40–5:00	Preparation for going home

another, what is wrong with shortening their play by a few minutes? It's the rhythm and the structure of the day that are important.

Where are the reading, writing, and talking in this schedule? These activities must be incorporated into every part of the day. During whole-group times, the teacher engages all the children in thinking, talking, reading, and writing about ideas related to the topic under study. The teacher reads aloud, tells stories, records the children's words on chart paper, engages the children in singing songs or reciting poems, presents new materials, and leads the children in a discussion. In activity time, the children move from one **literacy-enriched setting** to another, exploring the provided materials independently and with peers.

Whole-Group Time

• • • • • • • • • • • • • • • •

Dee's preschool class is about to gather on the rug for the day's first large-group time. Today, Dee is sharing a Big Book, *Tabby Tiger, Taxi Driver* (Cowley, 2002). She calls the children to the rug by clapping and calling out, "It's time to read a Big Book, a Big Book, a Big Book." The children clap along and join her on the rug. Dee starts group time by asking, "How many claps did we do in that sentence? I'll clap. You count." With the help of the classroom aide and Dee clapping slowly, the children arrive at the number 13. Dee responds, "Wow! Thirteen words in that sentence! Now you clap, and I'll count." The children clap and Dee counts, making a mark on the chart paper for each word. "Yep! You are right! Thirteen words in that sentence." Dee just introduced a **phonological awareness** skill to her young students. She also used the words *sentence* and *word*, two important reading concepts that her young students will need to understand.

At the front of the class, Dee has posted a piece of chart paper with the question, How do you get to school? She reads it as she points to each word. Ricardo shouts, "Walk." Dee responds, "So you use your (_____)." Ricardo says, "Feets." Under the question, Dee draws a picture of two feet and writes and says *feet*. She then asks, "How do you get to school?" Various children tell how they come to school, and Dee draws a picture and writes the label. "Today's story is about a way to get to school that none of you said; it's about a taxi. What's a *taxi*?" As Dee talks, she shows the children a picture of a taxi with the word *taxi* written under the picture. The children study the picture and several say, "It's a car." Dee responds, "Right—it is a special kind of car. What makes it special?" The children guess the "bump" on the top or the color. Dee tells the children that a taxi is a car that you have to pay to ride in. Dee has added the word *taxi* to the children's vocabulary and decided that she needs to invite a taxi driver to come to the center to build the children's background knowledge. She has begun to give children a context for understanding the story.

Dee turns the children's attention to the Big Book, *Tabby Tiger, Taxi Driver*. She begins by reading the cover page, underlining the words with her hand as she says and reads, "The title of this book is *Tabby Tiger, Taxi Driver.* The author is Joy Cowley. The illustrator is John Nez." She turns to the inside cover page and prompts the children, asking what they think the story will be about. They respond. Dee evaluates. "That's a great guess." She expands on the children's suggestions. Then, Dee turns the page and begins reading, tracking the print from left to right and pointing to each word as she reads. Dee has introduced the children to important print awareness concepts and has helped them begin to interact with and comprehend the text. She has demonstrated that readers make predictions about the text before they begin reading.

As Dee is reading the book, she stops often to engage the children in conversation. She *prompts* the children, asking them what they think will happen with Mr. Elephant's hot dog stand. They predict that Tabby Tiger will "bang it up." She *evaluates*, offering reinforcement for a good guess. She asks the children to *repeat* what happened.

Following Dee's reading of the book, she and the children discuss the story. Dee asks questions such as "Where did Tabby Tiger take the people who hailed her taxi?" "What kind of truck pulled the taxi out of the water?" "What did Tabby Tiger learn about driving a taxi?" "Would you want to take a ride with Tabby Tiger?"

● ● ● ● ● ● ● ● ● ● ● ● ● ● ●

Dee has conducted a whole-group time that promotes the literacy growth of all the children in her class. She has extended children's understanding of phonological awareness and important book concepts. And she has engaged the children in a lively and meaningful book discussion, adding words from the story to their vocabulary.

Activity Time

During activity time, the children played in the Taxi Play Center, hailing taxis, driving to various destinations, paying, and receiving receipts from the driver. The children also "read" maps and moved cars along them in the block center. In the **writing center**, they made license plates and made **environmental print** signs for use in the Taxi Play Center. They read books on transportation in the library center.

Why the long block of time for activity time and the shorter block of time for whole-group time? Young children need a generous uninterrupted block of time for play. It takes considerable time for them to plan their play with their peers, to negotiate roles with each other, and to carry out their play ideas. Children generally require from 30 minutes to an hour to develop and act out a single play scenario. The best play scenarios evolve over several days, with children resuming and extending their play each day.

In the past, teachers were advised that whole-group times needed to be short because young children's attention spans are short. Although it is true that young children find it challenging to sit for a long period of time, children's attention spans are remarkably long when they are engaged in an activity of interest to them.

Young children need time to move and time to sit; time to participate in individual, small-group, and large-group activities; and time for both teacher-directed and child-selected explorations.

Effective preschool teachers embed reading, writing, talking, and listening into every component of the daily schedule. They provide children with long blocks of time for individual and small-group activities and shorter blocks of time for whole-group gatherings. Effective teachers consider children's level of engagement as they guide the day's activities. They move on to something new when children are not working well together and allow extra time for exploration when something captures children's interest.

If you observe these scheduling principles in use in a classroom, congratulate the teacher. This teacher has created a schedule that maximizes the children's learning time.

CHAPTER 4

Helping Parents Help Their Children Learn

Although teachers are undeniably influential in promoting young children's literacy growth, they cannot go it alone. Parents are essential partners in their children's development of reading, writing, and talking skills. The research on early literacy development suggests not only how teachers can support children's learning in the classroom but also how they can support parents as first teachers at home. Building skilled and confident readers and writers requires collaboration between school and home, teachers and parents.

Strategies for Partnering With Parents

Encourage Parents to Talk With Their Children

Daily activities offer rich opportunities for vocabulary development when parents take the time to discuss the sights and sounds encountered along the way. For instance, a visit to the produce department of the grocery store can become an impromptu vocabulary lesson when parents explore the sizes, shapes, textures, and names of the various fruits and vegetables. What are the differences between Golden Delicious and Macintosh apples? How did the spaghetti squash get its name?

Like a daily vitamin, at least one new vocabulary word a day is a healthy habit. The key is for teachers to help parents understand the importance of talking with their children—to label what they see and discuss how it works. Remember, "Children who do not hear a lot of talk and who are not encouraged to talk themselves often have problems learning to read" (Armbruster, Lehr, & Osborne, 2003).

Encourage Families to Play With Words

• • • • • • • • • • • • • • • •

A parent and child are riding the bus home. The parent sees a stop sign and points it out to the child.

Parent: What rhymes with *stop*? *Pop, top, mop, bop, hop....*

(Before saying each rhyming word, the parent pauses and waits for the child to say the next word. The parent sees a police officer, points, and pauses.)

Child: Cop!

Parent: WOW! You made a rhyme! *Cop. Stop.*

Child: Fop!

Parent: Wow, are you good at making rhyming words!

● ● ● ● ● ● ● ● ● ● ● ● ● ● ● ●

When families play word games such as this, they discover that language can be a source of fun. In the beginning, the adult player will need to model the game and provide most of the rhyming words. But over time, as children gain more practice, they will learn to recognize and produce rhymes. Remind families that in rhyming games, sound is more important than meaning. Nonsense words are fine—and children enjoy them most of all.

Help Parents Help Their Children Learn About Books and Print

The National Education Goals Panel (1997) stated,

> Early, regular reading to children is one of the most important activities parents can do with their children to improve their readiness for school, serve as their child's first teacher, and instill a love of books and reading. Reading to children familiarizes them with story components such as characters, plot, action, and sequence ("Once upon at time...," "...and they lived happily ever after"), and helps them associate oral language with printed text. Most important, reading to children builds their vocabularies and background knowledge about the world. (p. 20)

The National Education Goals Panel also reported that only about 56% of 3- to 5-year-olds are read to daily by their parents. To ensure every child's success as a reader, this statistic has to change. There is so much that parents can be helped to do during storybook reading. For example, teachers can introduce parents to the PEER and CROWD storybook reading procedures described in chapter 1.

Encourage Parents to Talk With Their Children While Reading a Story

Talk helps young children understand stories and relate them to their own lives. Through discussion, stories become more meaningful. The following example demonstrates how talk can enrich the read-aloud experience:

● ● ● ● ● ● ● ● ● ● ● ● ● ● ● ●

Four-year-old Lauren and her mother are reading *The Biggest, Best Snowman* (Cuyler, 1998). The story begins with Little Nell's family telling her that she can't help because she is too small, so she goes off to play with her friends in the woods. Little Nell's friends ask her to help them build a snowman. Little Nell says that she can't help because she is too small.

Lauren's mother reads the first five pages and stops just after Bear Cub asks Little Nell to show the animals how to make a snowman.

Mother: So, what do you think Little Nell will say?

Lauren: I can't. I'm too little.

Mother: What makes you think Little Nell will say that?

Lauren: Because her name is *Little* Nell.

Mother: But you are little and you can do lots of things, can't you? Could you help the animals make a snowman? Let's see what Little Nell says.

As Mother continues reading, she stops regularly to ask questions and give feedback and to help Lauren connect the story to personal experiences. For example, after the bottom snowball is made, she asks, "What does the snowman need now?" and later, "Do you remember when you and Grandpa made a snowman last winter? Did you make your snowman just like Little Nell and her friends?" But Mother didn't ask all the questions.

Lauren: Why did they make the face using that stuff? What's that [gazed]? What's that [creation]?

And the storybook reading ended with Mother asking the last question:

Mother: So, what do you think BIG Mama, BIG Sarah, and BIG Lizzie learned about Little Nell?

● ● ● ● ● ● ● ● ● ● ● ● ● ● ● ●

Through many experiences reading many different kinds of books, Lauren is learning a lot about books and print. She knows how to hold a book. She knows that her mother reads the words in books, not the pictures. She knows that her mother reads the left page before reading the right page. Lauren is developing **concepts of print**.

What kinds of books should teachers encourage parents to read to their children? The same kinds that we recommend for the classroom library corner (see chapter 2): picture storybooks, predictable books, counting books, and informational books. Parents can begin by taking their children to the local library to take advantage of the many free resources available there.

Encourage Parents to Teach Children About Letters and Words

Children who have had experiences with print understand that the squiggly marks on paper are special; they can be named. Repeated exposure and varied experience are the keys to building alphabet knowledge. Parents can support this learning in many ways. One of the most important ways is by helping children learn the names of the letters of the alphabet, beginning with those letters in the child's name. At the same time, parents should understand that children develop at different rates and that not all children will be able to name the letters of the alphabet by the time they are 5. Marilyn Adams (1990) suggests beginning with uppercase letters, followed by lowercase letters. Uppercase letters are likely to be more familiar to children because they see more uppercase letters in the world outside the classroom.

> Repeated exposure and varied experience are the keys to building alphabet knowledge.

Teachers can suggest many simple activities for parents to share with their children, such as singing the alphabet song, looking for letters in street signs and license plates, writing children's names and naming each letter in turn, finding letters in books and newspapers, and reading alphabet books.

Children can begin to recognize words at the same time they are learning about letters; it is not necessary for children to know the names of the letters before they learn to identify highly meaningful words. Teachers might recommend that parents read predictable books with repeated phrases and read these books again and again. While reading, parents should point to the words and encourage their children to chant the repeated phrases with them. In the following scene, Quinn and his father share a bedtime ritual.

• • • • • • • • • • • • • • • •

Quinn's favorite book is *Brown Bear, Brown Bear, What Do You See?* (Martin, 1992). Every night he yells, "Brown Bear, Brown Bear!" to indicate his bedtime reading choice. His father groans; Quinn giggles. Daddy says, "Okay, but only if you read it with me." Quinn's father reads the "...What do you see?" pages, and Quinn "reads" the "I see a..." pages. Daddy is often heard to say, "Quinn, you are one heck of a reader!"

• • • • • • • • • • • • • • • •

Quinn's enthusiastic reading of *Brown Bear, Brown Bear, What Do You See?* occurred because his father read the book to him many times. The book's repeating pattern supported Quinn's efforts to "read" with and to his father. Such books make it easy for parents to say, "What a good reader you are!"

Remember the earlier discussion of children's reading of **environmental print** (e.g., cereal names, soft drink names, road signs, and billboards)? Drawing attention to environmental print is another key way in which parents can support their children's ability to recognize meaningful words.

There is one more word of great importance to each preschooler: his or her name. Teachers might encourage parents to print their child's name on a piece of paper and post it above his or her bed, on the refrigerator, and in other visible places in the home. Writing the child's name while he or she watches, saying each letter as it is written, and asking the child to say the letters and read the name will help children begin to recognize this very important word.

Helping Parents Become "First Teachers"

Teachers can teach parents in many different ways. Parent–teacher interactions provide parents with information on how to support their children's literacy learning and give teachers information on how to extend the children's home-based learning in the classroom. Home visits and parent workshops are two kinds of personal interactions many preschool teachers use.

Home Visits

While some home-visit programs are simply visits to children's homes, others combine home visits with instruction. These programs can have a lasting effect on young children's development. Home-visit programs help parents see themselves as their children's first and most important teachers. Take a look at a typical home visit:

● ● ● ● ● ● ● ● ● ● ● ● ● ● ● ●

Tyrone's teacher visits his home once every other week on Monday. On Tuesday through Thursday, Tyrone plays and learns in a preschool classroom with his teacher and 14 peers. On this Monday, his teacher arrives at his home planning to read *Chicka Chicka Boom Boom* (Martin & Archambault, 1989). She begins by reading the storybook to Tyrone while his grandmother watches. The teacher pauses to focus Tyrone's attention on the pictures, to ask him to predict what might happen next, to invite him to "read" a word with her, and so forth. Following the reading, she gives Tyrone a sheet of paper, several paper scraps, and some paste to make a collage picture. As Tyrone works at making the collage, the teacher and grandmother talk about his development as a reader and a writer. The teacher asks the grandparent about Tyrone's interest in letters and words. Does he ask her the names of letters and words? Does she help Tyrone notice the letters and words on signs and food packages? When Tyrone is finished with his collage, the teacher helps him print his name on the paper. Tyrone prints the initial *T* and the teacher writes the rest, announcing the letters as Tyrone watches. She finishes by writing *Tyrone is a collage artist!* Tyrone displays his artwork on the refrigerator. Finally, the teacher leaves Tyrone and his grandmother with several storybooks and some suggestions for related activities.

● ● ● ● ● ● ● ● ● ● ● ● ● ● ● ●

For any home-visit program to be successful, the teacher and parents must speak the same language. If the teacher is not conversant in a child's home language, inviting another adult who speaks both the teacher's and the parents' language to assist in the home visit can help to facilitate communication.

Parent Workshops

When teachers teach all day every day, it can be difficult to find time to visit the children's homes. Parent workshops are an efficient way for teachers to meet with families and share suggestions and techniques for supporting children's literacy development at home. During workshops, instead of demonstrating to one parent, the teacher models teaching strategies for everyone in attendance. By providing access to engaging materials and demonstrating how to use them, teachers can help parents become partners in their children's learning.

What topics should workshops address? As we've seen in the previous pages, parents are most effective as first teachers when they concentrate on three goals: talking with children, helping children learn about books and print, and teaching children about letters and words. Effective preschool family workshops should focus on these three goals.

Sponsoring a successful parent workshop requires careful planning. Ask yourself, What activities will work best with these parents? (Remember: Parents are most engaged when they are active participants. Interactive activities are more effective and enjoyable than lectures.) What supplies are needed? How should the meeting room be organized? What time works best for the parents? Are there funds for refreshments? Are name tags needed? Who will provide child care?

No matter how carefully planned the workshop is, not all the children's parents will attend. Therefore, preschool teachers must look for other ways to involve their children's families.

Other Ways to Involve Families

Some preschool teachers send letters to their children's homes with specific suggestions for activities parents and children can share (see Figure 7).

Figure 7
Sample Parent Letter

Dear Merrie,
Have you been wondering why I have been asking the children to bring in an empty cereal box? Well, we are making a classroom display of our favorite cereals. We cut the front from each cereal box and glue it to a piece of posterboard. Every morning we read the names of our favorite cereal. The children are reading environmental print.

What is environmental print? It is the real-life print children see everywhere they look. Environmental print can be found on street signs ("STOP"), store signs ("Pizza Hut"), and food packages ("Cheerios"). Because the location of the print gives clues to its meaning, environmental print is often the first type of print young children can recognize and understand.

Why not take a walk with your child in your neighborhood to look for environmental print? Take along a pad of paper. Sketch the location of the environmental print and write the word just like it appears (e.g., *STOP*). Back home, see how many environmental print words you and your child can read. Staple the pages together and make a cover for your environmental print book. Encourage your child to "read" your special book to you and other family members.

Sincerely,
Carol

Some teachers also prepare backpacks with book and learning activities that children can check out for use at home. For example, teacher Lynn Cohen (1997) has developed 20 backpacks, each on a different theme, author, or genre (e.g., poetry, nonfiction, memoirs). Topics include folk tales and fairy tales, the post office, birthdays, and more. Each backpack contains books for the children, a book for the parents, and a notebook in which family members can share their thoughts about the book. Parents are encouraged to read the books and talk about them with their children. Carolyn Lingo, another teacher, sends home backpacks that include storybooks with related activities and hands-on materials. For example, one of her backpacks is based on *Mouse Paint* by Ellen Stoll Walsh (1995). It contains small vials of paint and mixing cups, a paintbrush, a smock, and a newspaper to cover the table. A brief note instructs parents to read the book with their child and then to mix the yellow, blue, and red paints, just like the mice in the book do. Parents and children are encouraged to describe what happened.

Lynn and Carolyn, like many other teachers of young children, clearly know how important families are to their young children's reading, writing, and speaking development. Alone, teachers are challenged to support children's learning. Together, teachers and parents can support each other's efforts to build successful readers.

CHAPTER 5

Tying It All Together: Standards, Instruction, and Assessment

In recent years, curriculum **standards** have gained tremendous influence in both K–12 and pre-K education. What are standards? How did they come to be developed? And how will standards affect how preschool teachers assess their young children's learning? Preschool teachers have many questions about this new development in early childhood education.

Some early literacy educators and policymakers see standards as a threat. They worry that establishing pre-K standards will result in the primary-grade curriculum being pushed down into preschool programs, requiring teachers to teach to the standards in ways that are not appropriate for young children. They argue that how young children learn is different from how older children learn and that different types of instruction are needed for the two age groups.

But other early educators and policymakers believe that standards that are developed on a solid research base can be very useful to preschool teachers. Early literacy educators can use standards to guide their curriculum, instruction, and **assessment**. Standards define what children need to know, making it easier for teachers to decide what to teach. Because they want to know if their children are learning what is taught, teachers will know what to assess. In other words, the curriculum, the instruction, and the assessment will be aligned. When this alignment occurred in K–12 education, students' achievement improved (Smylie, Lazarus, & Brownlee-Conyers, 1996). The hope is that when pre-K standards are in place, young children's learning will be enhanced.

What Are Standards?

Standards tell teachers what knowledge and skills children should attain in a particular area, such as literacy or mathematics, by a particular time, such as the end of the pre-K years. Standards are child outcome statements.

Typical preschool standards might state, By the end of the pre-K years, a child should be able to

- name the main characters in a story when asked, "Who is in this story?";
- name many uppercase letters; and
- respond to his or her name, when called.

Because the early childhood field has been hesitant to use the word *standards*, these child outcome statements have been called by many different names. Sometimes they are called *building blocks, learnings, guidelines,* or *goals.*

Standards are most valid and effective when they are developed from a solid research base. A growing body of research informs early childhood educators about what children need to know before coming to school if they are to be successful readers and writers. Two important summaries of this research suggest sets of research-based outcomes or accomplishments that successful learners are likely to exhibit during the preschool years (International Reading Association [IRA] & National Association for the Education of Young Children [NAEYC], 1998; Snow et al., 1998):

Birth to Age 3

- Pretends to read books
- Labels objects in books
- Produces letterlike forms and scribbles with some features of English writing
- Recognizes specific books by cover

Ages 3 and 4

- Recognizes local environmental print
- Knows that it is the print that is read in stories
- Uses new vocabulary and grammatical constructions in own speech
- "Writes" (scribbles) message as part of playful activity
- Demonstrates via questions and comments understanding of literal meaning of story being told

In 2003, another committee, the National Early Reading Panel, was established to study the evidence-based research on the development of early literacy in young children. This panel sought to identify the skills and abilities of young children from birth to 5 years of age that predict later achievement in reading. The panel's preliminary findings suggest that the following variables are critical to young children's later success as readers (D. Strickland, personal communication, January 20, 2004):

Oral Language Development
• Expressive and receptive vocabulary

Alphabetic Code
• Alphabet knowledge
• Phonological and phonemic awareness
• Invented spelling

Print Knowledge
• Environmental print
• Concepts of print

Other Skills
• Rapid naming of letters and numbers
• Visual memory and visual–perceptual abilities

These skills and abilities define what young children should know and be able to do by the end of the pre-K years and serve as a foundation for the development of state early literacy standards.

In 2002, the U.S. federal government launched an early childhood initiative known as *Good Start, Grow Smart*. At the heart of *Good Start, Grow Smart* was the concern that not all young children are receiving quality education and care, not even those young children in federally supported preschool programs. This initiative sought to "help States and local communities strengthen early learning for young children...[in order to] ensure that young children are equipped with the skills they need to start school ready to learn" (White House, 2002). One component of this initiative was to encourage states to develop voluntary guidelines on language and prereading skills for children ages 3 to 5 that align with each state's K–12 standards. To date, more than half the states have heeded this call and have established oral language and early literacy standards.

Judith Schickedanz (in press) studied early literacy guidelines in 15 states in order to create a single list of standards. A revised version of Schickedanz's composite list of accomplishments appears in Appendix B.

From Standards to Instruction

• • • • • • • • • • • • • • • •

It's September, and Jodie, a newly hired Head Start teacher in Virginia, is as excited and nervous as her 4-year-old students. In preparation for her children's arrival, Jodie read everything the center director gave her. One document was *Virginia's Foundation Blocks for Early Learning: Guidelines for Literacy and Mathematics* (Virginia Department of Education, 2003). She read that the purpose of the Virginia standards document was "to provide early childhood educators a set of basic guidelines in literacy and mathematics with indicators of success for entering kindergarteners based on scientifically based research" and that the guidelines had been aligned with the state's kindergarten standards. She carefully studied each of the **specific indicators**—outcomes such as, the child can successfully

- detect beginning sounds in words,
- listen to 2 one-syllable words and blend them together to form the compound word,
- identify words that rhyme, and
- generate simple rhymes.

She compared the Virginia guidelines with the Head Start Framework Outcomes to understand the overlap between these two sets of guidelines. By studying these documents, Jodie figured out what her students would be expected to know by the end of their year with her.

One of the Virginia standards specifies that by the end of preschool children should be able to demonstrate that they can correctly identify 10 to 18 uppercase alphabet letters by name in random order. Jodie knows that she needs to plan activities that provide her young learners with the opportunity to learn the names of the letters of the alphabet. She also knows that she wants the activities she provides to be developmentally appropriate for her young learners. *Virginia's Foundation Blocks for Early Learning* suggests a music activity that provides Jodie's students with an opportunity to learn the names of the letters of the alphabet.

Jodie begins by making large letter cards on 8½ by 11-inch paper. She prints one letter (both upper- and lowercase) on each card. Because there are 15 children in her group, she selects 15 of the large letter cards. Because it is early in the year and because she knows that the letters in their names are the most important letters to young children, the 15 letters include the first letter in each student's name.

Jodie continues by placing the letter cards in a circle on the floor. She tells the children that she will be playing music. While the music is playing, they are to march around the letter cards. When the music stops, each child is to stop and pick up a card. Each child will show the card to the group and say the name of the letter. Jodie and her aide do a quick demonstration of how the game is played.

The music begins, the children march, the music stops, and the children stop and pick up the letter in front of them. Each child shows the letter to the group and says or guesses its name. If a child identifies the letter correctly, Jodie says, "Good job! It's the letter __! If the child guesses incorrectly, she says, "Good guess, Anthony! Can anyone help Anthony name the letter?" She calls on the children to "show and name" the letters. To keep the activity fresh, she reviews only a few letter names in each round, concentrating on the children who have chosen the first letter in their name. Then, the children put the letter cards back on the floor, and the music begins again.

• • • • • • • • • • • • • • • •

Notice the playfulness of this activity. Early educators have long invited children to march to music. Today, early educators like Jodie are encouraged to embed what their students need to know and be able to do into typical early childhood activities. By infusing old activities with new content, preschool teachers can provide developmentally appropriate opportunities for children to develop the knowledge and skills addressed in performance standards.

Take another look at the description of Dee's storybook reading activity in chapter 3. This description provides another illustration of an early literacy educator teaching vocabulary, oral expression skills, phonological awareness, print and book concepts, and comprehension skills, all in one group time.

From Standards to Instruction and Assessment

Standards, instruction, and assessment need to be intricately intertwined. That is, children should be assessed on what the standards indicate they need to know and be able to do. To assess children on material that they have had little or no opportunity to learn would be unfair and inappropriate. Hence, standards, instruction, and assessment must all be linked together. When teachers know the standards, they know what to teach and what to assess.

Assessment, then, is the gathering of relevant information to document a child's learning and growth. What skills should teachers assess? They should assess the skills specified in the standards. Assessment provides the teacher with the means and data to answer questions about how close the child is to achieving—or meeting—each standard.

Gathering the Assessment Data

Teachers need to use multiple measures to gather sufficient information and get an accurate picture of the child's learning and growth. Two kinds of assessment, **informal assessment** and **formal assessment**, can be used for this purpose.

Informal Assessment.   Most of the assessments that early educators use are informal. In fact, the IRA/NAEYC (1998) position statement on developmentally appropriate practices for young children suggests

> early reading and writing cannot simply be measured as a set of narrowly defined skills on standardized tests. These measures often are not reliable or valid indicators of what children can do in typical practice, nor are they sensitive to language variations, culture, or experiences of young children (Johnston, 1997; Shepard, 1994; Shepard & Smith, 1988). Rather, a sound assessment should be anchored in real-life writing and reading tasks and continuously chronicle a wide range of children's literacy activities in different situations. (p. 14)

Informal assessments are typically called *authentic assessments* because these data are gathered while children engage in everyday classroom activities and real-life literacy tasks. Informal assessment relies on the teacher's ongoing collection of artifacts and information to illustrate children's knowledge and learning. Such artifacts include notes written by the teacher describing the child's behavior (called *anecdotal notes*), checklists, teacher–child interview responses, survey data, video or audio recordings of the child, and samples of the child's work. Often, these artifacts are housed in a collection called a *portfolio*. Take a look at how informal assessment enabled one teacher to answer the question, "How are the children doing?"

• • • • • • • • • • • • • •

Jodie planned to use the alphabet letter music activity to assess her children's knowledge of alphabet letter names. She made a grid with the letter names across the top and her children's names down the side. When a child provided the correct letter name, the classroom aide put the date in the appropriate box. Jodie used an informal assessment tool to gather important information about her children's knowledge of alphabet letter names.

• • • • • • • • • • • • • •

Formal Assessment.   One problem with informal assessment is that teachers have to wait for behaviors to occur in the course of everyday classroom activities. Teachers sometimes need to hurry things along a bit in order to gain the information they need to plan effective literacy instruction. They can do this using formal assessment. Formal assessments can be developed by the teacher (e.g., asking a child to name randomly ordered alphabet letters), or they can take the form of a published early literacy assessment. In published assessments, the procedures, such as how long the child can take to answer the question, appropriate prompts, or hints that can be given the child, are standardized and held constant. This facilitates comparing a child's performance to the performance of other children.

Making Judgments

Simply gathering information is not sufficient. Both informal and formal assessments require that teachers make sense of the data. Teachers need to make professional judgments about the child's learning and development. The key questions are, Is the child making progress toward meeting the standard? What can the child do today that he or she could not do before?

Making Instructional Decisions

The goal of all assessment is to "help teachers tailor appropriate instruction to young children and to know when and how much intensive instruction on any particular skill or strategy might be needed" (IRA & NAEYC, 1998, p. 14).

Teachers assess children so that they are able to plan instruction that will meet the needs of each child. Notice how Jodie uses assessment data in the following example.

● ● ● ● ● ● ● ● ● ● ● ● ● ● ● ●

Jodie studied the checklist and made a list of the children who seemed to know the name of the initial letter in their first name. She then made a list of the children who seemed not to know the letter name. She made a special note about José and Martha. During the activity, she recalled that they would look at their card and say, "Boy!" or "Three." Jodie's tentative judgment was that they did not know the names of the letters of the alphabet, nor did they understand the concept of alphabet letters. She then began to plan alphabet activities that would be appropriate for all her young learners. She planned some group activities like the music activity. She planned to put some alphabet games into the manipulative center and to invite small groups of children to play these games with her during activity time. She also brainstormed a list of alphabet materials to add to other centers in the classroom.

● ● ● ● ● ● ● ● ● ● ● ● ● ● ● ●

The standards movement that made changes to K–12 education is now transforming preschool education. Early childhood educators are learning how to attend to standards in their classrooms, how to use appropriate early literacy strategies to provide their learners with many opportunities to achieve the standards, and how to assess their young learners' learning and development. Like their K–12 colleagues, their standards, curriculum, and assessment will be aligned.

CHAPTER 6

New Challenges, New Opportunities

Today's preschool teachers and preschool children face new challenges and new opportunities. Recall the description of the new research that supports developmentally appropriate reading, writing, and talking strategies presented in chapter 1. The **emergent literacy** researchers of the 1980s and 1990s revealed how children observe print and its uses in everyday life, test their ideas, and revise them according to the feedback they receive from supportive parents and teachers. These researchers discovered how critical it is for teachers and parents to read frequently to children; to engage them in conversations about text, print, and books; and to provide opportunities for them to observe and interact with adults and other children as they write for real-life purposes. They learned that with repeated opportunities to engage in meaningful literacy activities, a great deal of interaction with adults and peers, and some incidental instruction, many children become conventional readers and writers. These findings challenged preschool teachers to ask themselves questions such as the following:

- Do I read to my students frequently?
- When I read, do I engage the children in talk about the stories and the print?
- How often do the children see me reading and writing? Am I modeling a variety of forms of literacy for the children?
- Am I providing the children with opportunities to use reading and writing materials in the classroom?
- As the children test their ideas about how print works, do I provide them with supportive feedback that helps them revise their ideas?
- Do I give children the time they need to interact with me, other adults, and one another in meaningful literacy activities?

Teachers who can answer these questions with a *yes* are providing their young learners with opportunities to engage in meaningful reading and writing activities.

But this is only a beginning. Two groups of researchers have been studying young children's literacy skills and the related appropriate classroom instruction practices. Because of the research methods used by one group, their work has come to be known as **evidence-based reading research (EBRR)**. These EBRR researchers concluded that to become successful readers and writers, children first needed to master the skills necessary for processing print. This research enriched the emergent literacy research findings by identifying the core knowledge and skills that young children must have to become successful readers. The work of Whitehurst (1992) and other researchers revealed that children's oral language skills, **phonological awareness**, and alphabet knowledge at preschool age are predictive of their reading achievement in the elementary grades. This research suggested that there is a specific sequence in children's acquisition of phonological awareness and that print awareness, which includes **concepts of print**, is positively correlated with children's reading ability in the primary grades. These findings challenged preschool teachers to ask themselves the following questions:

- Am I providing the children with opportunities to learn the names of the letters of the alphabet?
- Do I engage in word play with the children, helping them learn that oral language is composed of words and that words consist of syllables and sounds?
- Do I help children focus on the sounds of words so that they become familiar with rhyme and alliteration?

If preschool teachers are to provide successful early literacy instruction, they must first understand what skills and experiences young children need in order to become successful readers and writers.

The EBRR research also identified effective strategies for teaching these core literacy skills to young children. One of the most consistent research findings is that young children's phonological awareness and alphabet knowledge can be increased through explicit instruction. In the past, preschool teachers typically have not used explicit instruction with young children. Here, then, is a new challenge. Fortunately, it is possible for this instruction to take the form of games and other developmentally appropriate activities. (See, for example, chapter 5 for the description of Jodie's music activity that teaches letter names.)

It is clear that both the emergent literacy and EBRR perspectives make significant contributions to a well-rounded early literacy program. Children need many meaningful, social engagements with books, various forms of print, and writing. In addition, most children also need some explicit, developmentally appropriate instruction on phonological awareness, letter recognition, and vocabulary. Teachers, therefore, need to know and use instructional strategies from both perspectives.

But doing everything that is proposed in this book is only a beginning. Even teachers who provide all the right elements—literacy-rich classroom environments, play-related literacy activities, interactive storybook reading, appropriate forms of explicit instruction, and family literacy activities—face another challenge. Teachers need to provide their young learners with opportunities to learn the key literacy skills while studying meaningful topics.

Selecting Meaningful Topics

Reread the descriptions of the classroom literacy activities presented in this book. Did you notice that they are always embedded in the children's study of a topic about which they are curious, one that helps them better understand how their world functions? Teachers need to carefully select a topic of study and then consider ways to use that topic as a springboard for teaching key literacy concepts. Although children think they are simply studying vehicles, teachers know they are also learning about the names of vehicles, how vehicles make our lives better, and the challenges vehicles create. In addition, children are learning that print is read from left to right and from top to bottom, that words are made up of letters, and that some words have rhyming sounds. The challenge is to select topics that interest young children and to integrate literacy activities into the study of every meaningful topic.

How do preschool teachers make the right decisions about which topics are "meaningful topics" for young children? Lillian Katz and Sylvia Chard (1993) suggest that teachers use relevance to children's daily lives as the criteria to select topics appropriate for young children's study. Using this advice, Karen Wellhousen (1996) chose to study homes with her young learners: who lives in them, things to do at home, different kinds of home structures, different types of homes, different locations, and parts of homes. Susan Humphries of the Coombes County Infant School in Arborfield Cross, England, chose to study native plants with her young learners. The children participated in the life cycle of numerous plants, from the planting to the harvesting and eating. Nancy Edwards of Newark, Delaware, and her students studied ponds, watching tadpoles turn into frogs and the pond animals and plants awaken after the long winter. Investigations like these help young children make sense of the world in which they live. Furthermore, they create a powerful context for meaningful reading, writing, and conversation. It is natural for children's vocabulary to grow through such studies. The challenge for the preschool teacher is to weave explicit teaching of key literacy skills into everyday activities. Mindful teachers ask questions and make decisions such as these:

- While I'm reading to the children today, which print awareness skills will I focus on? Perhaps I'll use a Big Book and focus on print going from left to right across the page.
- As we name the different kinds of transportation we know today, should I focus on the names of the letters in one vehicle? I think I'll focus on the *t* in *taxi*.

Without such careful planning, integration of literacy skills into the study of meaningful topics might not happen. This is a challenge that every preschool teacher faces.

Where to Go From Here?

The greatest challenges bring forth the greatest opportunities: to understand and use effective literacy teaching strategies while engaging children in exciting, meaningful investigations; to integrate essential literacy skills into every aspect of the curriculum; and to begin to link **standards**, content, and **assessment** in a mindful, developmentally appropriate manner. This book sets forth the foundations. The rest is up to you.

Suggested Materials for Thematic Play Settings

Home Center

Babysitter instruction forms
Children's books
Cookbooks, recipe box
Junk mail
Magazines, newspapers
Message board
Notepads
Pencils, pens, markers
Product containers from children's homes
Sticky notes
Telephone book
Telephone message pads

Business Office

Calendar
Computer keyboard and monitor
File folders
Notepads
Order forms
Pencils, pens, markers
Stationery, envelopes, stamps
Telephone message pads
Typewriter
Wall signs (e.g., "Please Sign In")

Restaurant

Cookbooks
Menus
Notepads/order pads
Pencils, pens, markers
Price chart
Product containers
Receipts
Telephone book
Wall signs (e.g., "Pay Here")

Post Office

Address labels
Baskets labeled "First Class," "Third Class," and "Air Mail"
Junk mail
Pencils, pens, markers
Stamps
Stationery and envelopes
Wall signs (e.g., "Line Starts Here")

Grocery Store

Checkbooks
Notepads
Pencils, pens, markers
Product containers
Shelf labels for store areas (e.g., "Meat")
Wall signs (e.g., "Supermarket")

Veterinarian's Office

Appointment book
Labels with pets' names
Magazines
Pamphlets
Pencils, pens, markers
Pet care chart
Prescription forms
Telephone book
Wall signs (e.g., "Receptionist," "Waiting Room," "The Doctor Is In")

Airport/Airplane

Air sickness bags with printed instructions
Books, magazines
Calendar
Luggage tags
Maps
Pencils, pens, markers
Tickets
Travel poster
Wall signs (e.g., "Baggage Claim Area")

Library

Books
Library cards
Pencils, pens, markers
Shelf labels for books (e.g., "ABCs," "Animals")
Wall signs (e.g., "Quiet!")

Preschool Standards

Oral Language (Standard)

Areas and Indicators

Gestural Expression

Uses gestures alone to communicate

Uses gestures in combination with speech to communicate

Verbal Expression

Expresses feelings, needs, and ideas

Uses language to maintain relationships with others

Participates in conversation

Asks questions, explains, and gives directions

Helps generate and maintain scripts in sociodramatic play

Vocabulary and Background Knowledge

Uses new words encountered in stories in retellings

Uses new words from book or other contexts in conversations

Asks for names of unfamiliar objects and their parts

Asks, "What does that mean?" when hears unfamiliar word

Understands relationships among objects (e.g., apples and oranges are fruits; socks and dresses are items of clothing)

Understands processes and properties associated with objects, animals, and plants (e.g., plants and animals grow; rocks do not grow)

Adapted from Schickedanz, J. (in press)

State Standards Reviewed: Alabama, Arkansas, Colorado, Connecticut, Georgia, Illinois, Louisiana, Massachusetts, Missouri, New Jersey, Ohio, Pennsylvania, Texas

Standards listed represent accomplishments (i.e., what children should know and be able to do) by the end of the preschool period (i.e., at age 5 to 5 ½).

Listening (Attention to and Comprehension of Talk)

Responds to name when called

Attends to stories read aloud

Follows directions

Responds to verbal cues from partner in sociodramatic play

Takes turns in conversation and relates own comments to topic

Phonological Awareness

Learns quickly to recite interesting-sounding words from texts (e.g., "oonga boonga" and "bunka wunka") and expresses delight in playing with such words

Thinks of a word that rhymes with a word the adult provides

Thinks of a word that starts with the same sound as a word the adult provides

Segments first sound in a word when teacher asks, "What's the first sound we hear in *bird*?" (Child: "/b/."), or when the child is writing words (e.g., Child: "*Birthday*. /b/.")

Literacy (Standard)

Areas and Indicators

Print Awareness

Asks what words in books and in the environment say

Indicates meaning for marks created when writing

Print Conventions and Book Handling Knowledge

Holds books right side up and proceeds from front to back

Looks at left page before right page when going through a book

Knows cover of book and that title of book is found there

Runs finger left to right and top to bottom when "reading" print

Letter Name Knowledge

Names many uppercase letters

Knows the lowercase form of all letters in own name

Finds specific letters in words in the environment (signs, book titles, and so on)

Alphabetic Principle

Attempts to sound out print in the environment

Attempts to sound out words and to spell them (can isolate first letter)

Tells adults, "*A* is for *acorn*" or "*B* is for *banana*"

Knowledge of Text Structures

Names different kinds of texts (recipes, menus, signs, newspapers, greeting cards, letters, storybooks)

Relates events from familiar narrative texts, in sequence

Seeks information from nonfiction texts

Generates stories with basic story structure in dramatic play, and when dictating stories at writing center

Comprehension of Stories

Names main characters when asked, "Who is in this story?"

Retells a story by enacting roles in play, or with puppets

Retells stories using book as prompt

Relates some main events when asked, "What happens in this story?"

Relates book experiences to own life (e.g., "I am going to make angels in the snow, just like Peter.")

Uses own experiences to understand characters' feelings and motivations

Uses background knowledge to interpret story events

Links basic emotions of characters to their actions in story events

Interest in Books

Chooses often to look at books in book area

Checks out books from classroom lending library

Requests that favorite stories be read

Looks at information books provided in the science or the block area

Demonstrates sustained and focused engagement during story time

Beginning Writing

Writes for many purposes (signs, labels, stories, messages, and so on)

Frequently chooses writing area

Uses writing in blocks and dramatic play contexts

Writes own name, using good approximations to letters needed

Makes mock and actual letters and experiments with letter forms

Organizes writing linearly on a writing surface and goes from left to right and from top to bottom

Uses two kinds of letters when writing: "big" ones and "little" ones

Composes messages and dictates or writes these

Contributes to class writing projects

Experiments with making words by stringing letters together to look like words or by attempting to link sounds in words to specific letter names

REFERENCES

Adams, M.J. (1990). *Beginning to read: Thinking and learning about print.* Cambridge, MA: MIT Press.

Adams, M.J., Foorman, B.R., Lundberg, I., & Beeler, T. (1998). The elusive phoneme: Why phonemic awareness is so important and how to help children develop it. *American Educator, 22*(1–2), 18–29.

Ambruster, B.B., Lehr, F., & Osborne, J. (2003). *A child becomes a reader: Birth through preschool.* Portsmouth, NH: RMC Research Corporation.

Arnold, D.S., & Whitehurst, G.J. (1994). Accelerating language development through picture book reading: A summary of dialogic reading and its effect. In D. Dickson (Ed.), *Bridges to literacy: Approaches to supporting child and family literacy* (pp. 103–128). Cambridge, MA: Basil Blackwell.

Baghban, M. (1984). *Our daughter learns to read and write: A case study from birth to three.* Newark, DE: International Reading Association.

Barrentine, S.J. (1996). Engaging in reading through interactive read-alouds. *The Reading Teacher, 50,* 36–43.

Bodrova, E., & Leong, D. (2003, May). *Assessing the level of play in prekindergarten and kindergarten children in order to promote more mature play that supports literacy as well as learning in general.* Paper presented at the 48th annual convention of the International Reading Association, Orlando, FL.

Bruner, J. (1983). Play, thought, and language. *Peabody Journal of Education, 60*(3), 60–69.

Bruner, J. (1984). Language, mind, and reading. In H. Goelman, A. Oberg, & F. Smith (Eds.), *Awakening to literacy* (pp. 193–200). Portsmouth, NH: Heinemann.

Calkins, L.M. (1996). *The art of teaching writing.* Portsmouth, NH: Heinemann.

Clark, M. (1976). *Young fluent readers: What can they teach us?* London: Heinemann.

Clay, M. (1966). *Emergent reading behavior.* Unpublished doctoral dissertation, University of Auckland, Auckland, New Zealand.

Cohen, L.E. (1997). How I developed my kindergarten book backpack program. *Young Children, 52*(2), 69–71.

DeLong, A.J., Tegano, D.W., Moran, J.D., Brickey, J., Morrow, D., & Houser, T.L. (1994). Effects of spatial scale on cognitive play in preschool children. *Early Education and Development, 5*(3), 237–246.

Duke, N.K. (2000). 3.6 minutes per day: The scarcity of informational texts in first grade. *Reading Research Quarterly, 35,* 202–225.

Durkin, D. (1966). *Children who read early: Two longitudinal studies.* New York: Teachers College Press.

Durkin, D. (1987). *Teaching young children to read* (4th ed.). Boston: Allyn & Bacon.

Enz, B., & Christie, J. (1997). Teacher play interaction styles: Effects on play behavior and relationships with teacher training and experience. *International Journal of Early Childhood Education, 2,* 55–69.

Ericson, L., & Juliebö, M.F. (1998). *The phonological awareness handbook for kindergarten and primary teachers.* Newark, DE: International Reading Association.

Fractor, J.S., Woodruff, M.C., Martinez, M.G., & Teale, W.H. (1993). Let's not miss opportunities to promote voluntary reading: Classroom libraries in the elementary school. *The Reading Teacher, 46,* 476–484.

Gambrell, L.B. (2000, April). *Fostering comprehension.* Paper presented at the 45th annual convention of the International Reading Association, Indianapolis, IN.

Han, M., & Christie, J. (2001). Environmental factors in play: Space, materials, and time. *International Journal of Early Childhood Education, 7,* 149–162.

Holdaway, D. (1979). *The foundations of literacy.* Gosford, NSW, Australia: Ashton Scholastic.

Katz, L.G., & Chard, S.C. (1993). *Engaging children's minds: The process approach.* Norwood, NJ: Ablex.

International Reading Association & National Association for the Education of Young Children (IRA & NAEYC). (1998). *Learning to read and write: Developmentally appropriate practices for young children.* Newark, DE: Author; Washington, DC: Author.

McGee, L.M., Lomax, R., & Head, M. (1988). Young children's written language knowledge: What environmental and functional print reading reveals. *Journal of Reading Behavior, 20*(2), 99–118.

Morrow, L.M. (2005). *Literacy development in the early years: Helping children read and write* (5th ed.). Boston: Allyn & Bacon.

National Education Goals Panel. (1997). *Special early childhood report.* Washington, DC: Author.

National Institute of Child Health and Human Development. (2000). *Report of the National Reading Panel. Teaching children to read: An evidence-based assessment of the scientific research literature on reading and its implications for reading instruction* (NIH Publication No. 00-4769). Washington, DC: U.S. Government Printing Office.

Neuman, S.B. (2002). *What research reveals: Foundations for reading instruction in preschool and primary education.* Washington, DC: U.S. Department of Education.

Neuman, S.B., & Roskos, K. (1992). Literacy objects as cultural tools: Effects on children's literacy behaviors in play. *Reading Research Quarterly, 27,* 203–225.

Rayner, K., Foorman, B.R., Perfetti, C.A., Pesetsky, D., & Seidenberg, M.S. (2002). How should reading be taught? *Scientific American, 286*(3), 84–91.

Roskos, K., & Christie, J. (2001). Examining the play-literacy interface: A critical review and future directions. *Journal of Early Childhood Literacy, 1*(1), 59–89.

Schickedanz, J.A. (in press). A framework and suggested guidelines for prekindergarten content standards. *The Reading Teacher.*

Smylie, M.A., Lazarus, V., & Brownlee-Conyers, J. (1996). Instructional outcomes of school-based participative decision making. *Education Evaluation and Policy Analysis, 18*(3), 181–198.

Snow, C.E., Burns, M.S., & Griffin, P. (Eds.). (1998). *Preventing reading difficulties in young children.* Washington, DC: National Academy Press.

Snow, C., & Ninio, A. (1986). The contracts of literacy: What children learn from-learning to read books. In W. Teale & E. Sulzby (Eds.), *Emergent literacy: Writing and reading* (pp. 116–137). Norwood, NJ: Ablex.

Sulzby, E. (1985). Children's emergent reading of favorite storybooks: A developmental study. *Reading Research Quarterly, 20,* 458–481.

Sulzby, E. (1990). Assessment of emergent writing and children's language while writing. In L.M. Morrow & J. Smith (Eds.), *Assessment for instruction in early literacy.* Englewood, NJ: Prentice Hall.

Sulzby, E., & Teale, W. (1991). Emergent literacy. In R. Barr, M.L. Kamil, P. Mosenthal, & P.D. Pearson (Eds.), *Handbook of reading research* (Vol. 2, pp. 727–757). White Plains, NY: Longman.

Virginia Department of Education. (2003). *Virginia's foundation blocks for early learning: Guidelines for literacy and mathematics.* Retrieved February 9, 2004, from http://www.pen.k12.va.us/VDOE/Instruction/Elem_M/FoundationBlocks.pdf

Vukelich, C., Christie, J., & Enz, B. (2002). *Helping young children learn language and literacy.* New York: Allyn & Bacon.

Wellhousen, K. (1996). Be it ever so humble: Developing a study of homes for today's diverse society. *Young Children, 52*(1), 72–76.

White House. (2002). *Good start, grow smart: The Bush administration's early childhood initiative.* Retrieved February 9, 2004, from http://www.whitehouse.gov/infocus/earlychildhood/toc.html

Whitehurst, G.J. (1992). *How to read to your preschooler.* Paper prepared for the State of Connecticut Commission on Children.

Wien, C.A., & Kirby-Smith, S. (1998). Untiming the curriculum: A case study of removing clocks from the program. *Young Children, 53*(5), 8–13.

Yaden, D.B., Rowe, D.W., & MacGillivray, L. (2000). Emergent literacy: A matter (polyphony) of perspectives. In M.L. Kamil, P.B. Mosenthal, P.D. Pearson, & R. Barr (Eds.), *Handbook of reading research* (Vol. 3, pp. 425–454). Mahwah, NJ: Erlbaum.

Yaden, D.B., Smolkin, L., & MacGillivray, L. (1993). A psychogenetic perspective on children's understanding about letter associations during alphabet book readings. *Journal of Reading Behavior, 25*(1), 43–68.

Yopp, H.K. (1992). Developing phonemic awareness in young children. *The Reading Teacher, 45,* 696–703.

CHILDREN'S BOOK REFERENCES

Aylesworth, J. (2003). *Goldilocks and the three bears.* New York: Scholastic.

Baker, L.A. (2003). *The animal ABC.* New York: Henry Holt.

Chodos-Irvine, M. (2003). *Ella Sarah gets dressed.* San Diego: Harcourt.

Cobb, V. (2003). *I face the wind.* New York: HarperCollins.

Cowley, J. (2002). *Tabby Tiger taxi driver.* Bothell, MA: Wright Group.

Cox, J. (2003). *My family plays music.* New York: Holiday House.

Crews, D. (1997). *Truck.* New York: Greenwillow.

Cuyler, M. (1998). *The biggest, best snowman.* New York: Scholastic.

dePaola, T. (1977). *The quicksand book.* New York: Holiday House.

Flor, A.F., & Campoy, F.I. (2003) *¡Pío peep! Traditional Spanish nursery rhymes.* New York: HarperCollins.

Gibbons, G. (1988). *Tool book.* New York: Holiday House.

Greenfield, E. (1978). *Honey, I love.* New York: HarperCollins.

Jay, A. (2003). *ABC: A child's first alphabet book.* New York: Dutton.

Jenkins, S., & Page, R. (2003). *What do you do with a tail like this?* Boston: Houghton Mifflin.

Lee, D. (2002). *Sylvia's garage.* Bothell, WA: Wright Group.

Lehn, B. (2002). *What is an artist?* Brookfield, CT: Millbrook.

Martin, B., Jr. (1992). *Brown Bear, Brown Bear, what do you see?* New York: Holt.

Martin, B., Jr. & Archambault, J. (1989). *Chicka chicka boom boom.* New York: Simon & Schuster.

Morales, Y. (2003). *Just a minute: A trickster tale and counting book.* San Francisco: Chronicle.

Moses, W. (2003). *Will Moses' Mother Goose.* New York: Philomel.

Murphy, M. (2003). *I kissed the baby.* Cambridge, MA: Candlewick.

Pearson, D. (2003). *Alphabeep, a zipping, zooming ABC.* New York: Holiday House.

Recorvits, H. (2003). *My name is Yoon.* New York: Farrar, Straus & Giroux.

Rohmann, E. (2002). *My friend rabbit.* Brookfield, CT: Roaring Brook.

Scarry, R. (1999). *Best Mother Goose ever!* New York: Golden.

Sendak, M. (1962). *Chicken soup with rice.* New York: HarperCollins.

Siebert, D. (1984). *Truck song.* New York: HarperCollins.

Smith, W.J. (2003). *Up the hill and down: Poems for the very young.* Honesdale, PA: Boyds Mills Press.

Waddell, M. (2003). *Hi, Harry! The moving story of how one slow tortoise slowly made a friend.* Cambridge, MA: Candlewick.

Walsh, E.S. (1995). *Mouse paint.* San Diego: Harcourt.

INDEX

Note: Page numbers followed by *f* indicate figures.

K

L

M

N

Ninio, A., 8
nonfiction books, 1, 28–29

O

open-ended prompts, 17
oral language: and early literacy, 14–15; research on, 11; standards on, 53, 65
Osborne, J., 43

P–Q

Page, R., 28
parental involvement, 8, 43–50; and early literacy, 15–16; letter on, 49*f*; strategies for, 43–47
parents: as first teachers, 47–50
parent workshops, 48–49
Pearson, D., 28
PEER procedure, 16–17
Perfetti, C., 10–11
Pesetsky, D., 10–11
phonemic awareness, 2; definition of, vi; research on, 11–14
phonemic manipulation: early literacy activities with, 13
phonological awareness, 39, 60; definition of, vi; research on, 11; standards on, 66
planning: daily schedule, 37–41
play leaders: teachers as, 35
play settings: thematic, materials for, 63–64
portfolio, 57
Post Office play center: materials for, 63
preschool standards, 65–68
print: access to, 8; concepts of, v, 1, 6, 60; environmental, v, 7, 23–24, 47, 49*f*; knowledge of, standards on, 53; parents and, 44
print awareness: research on, 11; standards on, 66
print conventions: standards on, 66
print-rich environment: creating, 19–36
questions: on early literacy, 59–60; what, where, when, why, and how, 17

R

Rayner, K., 10–11
reading: learning, 5–18; tools for, in classroom, 30–31
reading tubs, 25–26
recall prompts, 17
Recorvits, H., 28
Restaurant play center: materials for, 63
rhyming: early literacy activities with, 12
Rohmann, E., 28
Roskos, K., 31–32

S

T

V